Aims, Methods and Assessment in Advanced Science Education

Edited by
D. E. Billing and B. S. Furniss

HEYDEN & SON LTD

London · New York · Rheine

Heyden & Son Ltd., Spectrum House, Alderton Crescent, London NW4 3XX.
Heyden & Son Inc., 225 Park Avenue, New York, N.Y. 10017, U.S.A.
Heyden & Son GmbH, Steinfurter Str. 45, 4440 Rheine/Westf., Germany.

ISBN 085501 072X

Printed by The Whitefriars Press Ltd., London and Tonbridge

Aims, Methods and Assessment
in
Advanced Science Education

Acknowledgments

We wish to thank Thames Polytechnic, and in particular its School of Chemistry and its Central Service Unit, for help in arranging the Conference on which this book is loosely based.

We are grateful to publishers and authors for permission to reproduce the following material. Bibliographic reference is given at the place in text where the material appears.

Table 2.3 by permission of The Institution of Electrical Engineers.

Table 2.6 by permission of Fearon Publishers.

Quotation (Blake) p. 16 by permission of C. S. Blake.

Quotation (Bloom) p. 17 by permission of David McKay Company Inc.

Quotations (Krathwohl) pp. 19, 20 by permission of David McKay Company Inc.

Quotation (Gowenloch) p. 23 by permission of The Chemical Society.

Quotations (Bennett) pp. 23-25 by permission of The Chemical Society.

Tables 4.1 & 4.2 by permission of the Confederation of British Industry.

Tables 4.3, 4.4 & 4.5 by permission of The Chemical Society.

Tables 4.5 & 4.6 by permission of the Association for Programmed Learning & Educational Technology.

Example (Hoare) p. 80 © 1967 John Wiley & Sons Inc. By permission.

Examples, pp. 84 & 85: Copyright © 1971 The Open University. By permission.

Example, p. 90: From *Programmed Problems in Thermodynamics* by E. Braun & E. T. Wait. Copyright © 1967 McGraw-Hill Publishing Company Limited.

Example, p. 91, by permission of The Nuffield Foundation.

Example, pp. 92 & 93, by permission of M. Harris.

Figure 11.1 by permission of the Division of Chemical Education, American Chemical Society.

Figures 11.3 & 11.4 by permission of A. J. Romiszowski.

Table 11.1 by permission of the Association for Programmed Learning & Educational Technology.

Table 14.2 by permission of Oregon State University Press.

Examples, p. 133. Copyright © 1971 The Open University. By permission.

Example (A-level paper) p. 137, by permission of School Examinations Dept.,
    University of London.
Example (C.S.E. paper) p. 137, reproduced by permission from Schools Council
    Examination Bulletin 21: *CSE: An Experiment in the Oral Examining of
    Chemistry* (Evans/Methuen Educational, London, 1971).

Contents

IV. Assessment Methods

V. Conclusions

VI. Appendices

Foreword

The problems and uncertainties facing science education at the post-school level in this and other countries at the present time are formidable.

First, there is the question of student numbers. There are unfilled places in science departments in most universities, polytechnics and colleges of education; and furthermore the knowledge, abilities and attitudes of those who do enter science courses are different to those of a few years ago (*different not worse*—the success of the various curriculum development projects at school level is now having its inevitable impact at the higher level).

Second, there is the employment situation. Many experts believe that there has been a permanent change from the position during the two decades immediately following World War II, when anyone with a science qualification could obtain a post involving science. Increasingly science graduates will need to seek, and will find, except in very adverse economic circumstances, employment in diverse occupations. Are the present degree courses suitable for the changed employment situation?

Third, one of the consequences of the current public disenchantment with science is that Governments will give less support for research. In common with other subjects it is also likely that the staff–student ratio will worsen.

Fourth, scientific knowledge has an ever increasing growth rate with the consequence that science courses have an overfull content. It is so easy to introduce new material, but so difficult to reduce a syllabus. Last, the boundaries between the various branches of science are becoming blurred, and some of the most important and rapidly expanding areas e.g. biophysics lie between the traditional subjects and so are sparsely covered.

All this leads science teachers, and also quite properly their students, to question the value and direction of science education today. What should be the philosophy behind science courses? What are their overall aims? Is a study of science to be looked upon as one of many possible vehicles for education—a preparation of the mind, or should science courses be planned to meet social and economic needs—a preparation for a career? Even if the overall aims can be agreed, how do a group of teachers set about translating these aims into specific objectives? What will these objectives imply for decisions about course content and teaching (or better, learning) method? How can

Dr. X be persuaded that the twenty lectures he has always given on subject Y are no longer required? Which of the bewildering array of educational techniques should be selected for a particular learning situation? Which methods of assessment should be used? These and many other questions are being asked, and this book gives, or points the direction to at least some of the answers.

Increasingly tertiary level science teachers are becoming aware of the problems, and many are giving time in an already over-full day to work towards finding the answers. What is needed now is more research; a greater understanding and recognition for those who decide to work on problems in science education; more properly planned conferences, such as the one which led to this book; coordination, nationally and regionally, of discussion groups and workshops; and easier dissemination of the results of research and innovation.

The editors and authors are to be congratulated on producing this timely and helpful book which will undoubtedly contribute to solving some of the current problems in educating people *through,* and *for,* science.

M. J. FRAZER
Professor of Chemical Education

February 1973   University of East Anglia

CHAPTER 1

Introduction

The need for changes in tertiary science education is becoming increasingly apparent. The exponential increase in scientific knowledge, the changes in the school syllabuses, the expansion of research and development work in tertiary science and the changing requirements of industry must all be taken into account in order to derive maximum benefit from such changes. Since it is not easy for the individual lecturer to keep abreast of the developments in scientific knowledge and at the same time to be fully aware of current work in the other areas mentioned above a survey of ideas and results in these areas is needed. This is particularly necessary in the rapidly expanding areas of educational research and educational technology which frequently cause suspicion, and occasionally hostility among scientists.

Accordingly, we organized a conference in December 1971 at Thames Polytechnic upon the theme of Developments in Tertiary Chemical Education. This book is a direct result, but it is only loosely based upon that conference. Although many of the examples used in the papers are taken from chemistry, it became obvious at the conference, and in editing the proceedings, that the concepts being discussed were of very general application within Science Education. The title *Aims Methods and Assessment in Advanced Science Education* reflects this generality. We have used the description 'advanced' to refer not only to tertiary (post 'A' level) courses, but also advanced secondary courses: the newer secondary courses are blurring the distinction between school and university work.

The aims of this book are to—

(*a*) review the salient features of research and innovation in advanced science education;

(*b*) emphasize the reasons for the interest in currently important areas of investigation;

(*c*) avoid jargon, but also to introduce scientists to the vocabulary and techniques of educational research;

(*d*) indicate current growth areas by reference to research findings.

The book, like the conference, has a structure based upon the simplified model of curriculum development shown in Fig. 1.1. Course design, according to the systematic approach, involves first specifying the objectives. Then the appropriate content of the

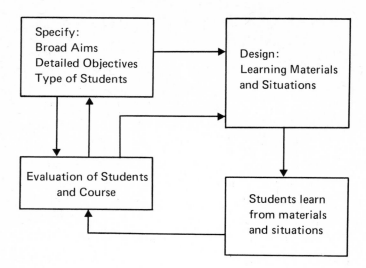

Fig. 1.1 A Curriculum Development Model

course and the teaching methods are selected; the design of learning situations
(lectures, tutorials, films, laboratory work etc.) and the construction of materials (e.g
booklets, films, TV programmes, etc.) follows. After the teaching, the students are
tested on the basis of criteria derived from the objectives. This testing allows the
student's abilities to be assessed, and also provides a 'feedback' of information which
can be used to improve the design of objectives, materials or learning situations.

The book therefore has four sections, dealing with objectives, design of materials
(curriculum developments), teaching and learning methods (educational techniques),
and assessment methods.

I. OBJECTIVES

CHAPTER 2

Objectives in Tertiary Science Education

R. BEARD

Fifteen years ago, it is unlikely that anyone would have attempted to discuss the aims of science education. No doubt every serious teacher had aims which he wished to see realized, but these were not analysed or extended to cover the whole range of teaching and evaluation of the subject. When asked to state their aims, university teachers might have answered 'to develop a habit of disciplined, rational thinking' or 'to enable students to study independently' but realization of these aims was not necessarily tested. Instead, there was a fairly common tendency to emphasize teaching methods and to set examinations which favoured those who memorized most effectively and who could marshall their thoughts rapidly; for instance, examinations consisted of writing notes or working familiar types of problem.

Since that time, the influence of Skinner (and those engaged in preparing programmed texts) has accustomed us to specifying objectives in some detail, to thinking about teaching methods in relation both to objectives and to students' needs, and to choosing methods of evaluation to determine whether the objectives are achieved. Table 2.1 shows commonly accepted objectives in university teaching, treated in this way. To achieve even this limited number of objectives, a diversity of teaching methods and of evaluation techniques is needed. In addition, changes in subjects and their content, in student numbers, their interests and qualifications and in professional requirements have had an influence on educational aims. Thus, the accelerating increase in knowledge makes it imperative that every student should be able to continue his own education after qualifying. This increase, together with growth in number of specialities, increases the need for a broadly based education in which general principles are emphasized.

The growth in team work, in research and committees, requires development of skills in communication and in interpersonal relationships. Table 2.2 lists these changes and suggests related objectives and methods to achieve them. Skill in self-education must be developed, so that students are able to continually update their knowledge, but this requires that they should learn in such a way that the whole structure of the subject is understood. An example of a co-operative project is the use—Black *et al.*—of

Table 2.1. Accepted Objectives in Higher Education

Commonly accepted objectives	Activities	Evaluation
Acquisition of the following:		
A habit of disciplined rational thinking	Essays; tutorials; criticism of experimental procedures	Viva; essays
Ability to study independently	Long essay; project	
Standards, modes of thought and skills appropriate to a field of study	All work in a course	Various. Examinations, etc.
Ability to apply knowledge in new situations	Open-ended questions; unfamiliar problems	
A critical approach to ideas and procedures	Discussion; tutorials	Shown in answers to questions inviting discussion and criticism

Table 2.2. Objectives Relevant to Recent Changes

Some Current Changes	Objective in Teaching	Teaching Activity
An accelerating increase in knowledge	Skill of self education obtaining information, etc. Emphasis on principles	Projects or long essays requiring students to seek information
An accelerating increase in the number of specialties	A broadly based education: emphasis on common principles. Flexibility in face of change	Introductory course emphasizing common principles. Projects relating to several fields of knowledge, etc.
Increasing need for co-operation in teams	To encourage skill in co-operation	Co-operative projects and activities. Group work designed to give insight into group relations
Greater importance of communication skills	To promote clarity and conciseness in written and oral communications	Criticism of essays and of written or verbal reports by students

'training groups' in the Physics Department at the University of Birmingham. The students worked together in groups of five and reported a feeling of 'sorting things out and learning' which they contrasted with that of 'knowing nothing' as a result of cramming for finals in the rest of the course. Skills in communication were also developed at Imperial College by Prosser, who found that mining students sent in considerably better reports if a member of staff discussed with them their methods and findings in open-ended experiments before the reports were written.

A specialist teaching his subject may tend to forget general aims of this kind. We, in the Unit, feel that it is essential to keep these in mind when specifying objectives for specialist courses. We have therefore worked out, for discussion and comment, some aims and general objectives, which should be achieved in university teaching (*see* Table 2.3).

Such aims, or long-term objectives, can be incorporated into a scheme of objectives for specialist studies. But, if the scheme is to be used, many other practical considerations relating to requirements and resources must be taken into account. The ratio of teachers to students and the availability of appropriate teaching skills influence the use of group methods; limitations of equipment such as books or audio-visual aids, and of technicians, space, or time available, correspondingly limit developments of new techniques for individual study; problems of administration may reduce choice of subjects; and traditional organization into specialized subject areas is likely to inhibit the introduction of integrated studies. Overall, rising costs tend to restrict developments in teaching since these still have low priority. For instance, there is no scheme of secondment for teachers in higher education to develop new teaching techniques.

OBJECTIVES IN A SPECIALIST FIELD

At the University Teaching Methods Unit, a study of objectives in physics was undertaken during 1968-71 by our Research Officer, Kay Pole, with a number of physicists in Surrey and London Universities and with other staff of the Unit. A preliminary outline of objectives, with related activities for students and methods of evaluation, was prepared in Surrey in 1969. The original statements, which were in many cases too general and inexact, have been elaborated under headings of 'knowledge', 'skills' and 'attitudes'. Typical entries are illustrated in Table 2.4.

In the full scheme, attitudes which should be fostered are also listed; e.g. 'a research attitude', 'enthusiasm for physics' and 'confidence in the scientific method'. These seem most likely to be realised in practical work, and in studies chosen by the students, such as projects. The scheme is not intended to be prescriptive but should serve as a basis for discussion, to stress the relationships between objectives, teaching methods and their evaluation, and to arouse interest in assessment of learning as it proceeds; it could apply almost in entirety to chemistry.

The value of specifying objectives in these ways is also shown by studies in which the content of a number of examinations were analysed. These show that the examinations teachers set are at variance with the aims they claim to uphold.

OBJECTIVES AND EXAMINATIONS

In studying objectives in teaching biochemistry, we have proceeded from an investigation into examinations, in preference to asking teachers what they hope to achieve or to studying teachers in action.[2]

In doing this, we have assumed that the range of cognitive skills tested in examinations is an indication of what examiners consider important. The bio-chemistry sub-committee of our Medical Research Committee decided that those who construct the

Table 2.3. Objectives in university education (for consideration and comment). (From *Electronics and Power*, March 1971)

Objectives	Teaching method or student activity	Evaluation or feedback
1. KNOWLEDGE At the end of a university career, a student should—		
know the basic terminology of his subject	Lectures; assigned reading; practicals; demonstrations etc.	Multiple-choice-question examinations; correct use of terms in essays, discussion etc.
know the principles (basic laws and concepts) of his subject	Lectures; assigned reading; practicals; demonstrations etc.	Correct reference to laws etc. in arguments; essay writing etc.
understand some of the uses to which his subject is put	Contact with research, industry, professionals in own field; experiments, projects, where appropriate	Informative assessment of project essays etc.
be acquainted with principles and applications of related subjects	General studies; background reading	Synthesis of data from various sources
2. SKILLS University teaching in general should enable the student—		
to write coherently	Essays; laboratory reports; dissertations; papers to be given in tutorials	Informative assessment of these
to be verbally articulate	Giving papers; effective argument in discussion groups; tutorials etc.	Criticism by other students and tutors
to make his own independent judgments	Meets contradictions; contrasting points of view; use of discussion to expose student's assumptions etc.	e.g. 'compare and contrast' questions in examinations; evaluation of arguments etc.

Table 2.3 cont.

to obtain information efficiently	Use of library, abstracts etc.; preparation for essays, projects; open-ended experiments	Informative comment on performance; open-book examinations
to think creatively, imaginatively and in abstract terms	Research projects; tackling unsolved problems; use of concepts in arguments, discussion	Quality of writing (publications?); assessment of method in tackling problems; credit for originality
to operate with colleagues and other professionals in future career	Joint projects; role playing; group discussion to give insight into group interactions	Evaluation of student's behaviour in a group by tutors and other students
to develop adaptability, i.e. to cope with changing patterns of knowledge (both general technological advance and new ideas in own subject)	Exposure to new ideas (not accepting everything given as 'facts')	Follow up after graduation
3. ATTITUDES An aim in university teaching is to foster in the student—		
enthusiasm for learning	Nonassigned reading; extracurricular meetings (e.g. science clubs)	Extent of extracurricular activity; posing new problems for own investigation
scholarly concern for accuracy	Contact with teachers and researchers displaying such accuracy; continuous checking of own results	Assign marks for accuracy in examinations
awareness of moral, social, economic, political and scientific problems of society	General studies; some projects; modern history, literature, sociology	Impressionistically, from student's writing and discussion

Table 2.4. Objectives in Teaching Physics

Objectives	Activities	Evaluation
KNOWLEDGE		
I.1 Knowledge of the language of physics —including: I.1.1 Scientific vocabulary I.1.2 Mathematical definitions I.1.3 Specialized use of ordinary language	I.1 Lectures Practicals Use of technical terms, formulae in problem-solving and writing	I.1 Traditional written examinations 'Points' tests (G) Correct use of technical terms, etc. in writing and discussion
I.5 Knowledge of experimental techniques and methods in the design and analysis of experiments	I.5 Formal laboratory work Open-ended experiments (G) Preparation for projects Work on project.	I.5 Assessment of laboratory reports Open book orals (G) Performance in discussion of project supervisor Assessment of project
SKILLS		
II.1 Collection of information II.1.1 Knowing where to find relevant information (from books, journals, notes, other students, teachers, etc.)	II.1 (a) on teachers' part Give sources of information in reading lists and bibliographies Frequent references to articles and journals in lectures	II.1 Are these followed up?

II.1.2 Skimming through the literature to find specified information	Lecture from librarian on use of library, abstracts and bibliographies	
II.1.3 Identifying important points and the evidence from them S	Set essays requiring information beyond that given in lectures	Are essays well-informed and based on several sources?
II.1.4 Finding structure in difficult material	*(b) on students' part* Expand lecture notes, e.g, to include information gained from reading	Indirect evidence from essays and essay type examination answers
	Give talk on a theme to discussion group	Discussion and criticism within group
	Write précis of difficult material	Assessment of précis
	Preparation for project	Supervisor's impressions during discussion on project
		Assessment of project

R. Beard

examinations should be invited to assign questions already set in their 1968 examination papers, to McGuire's categories. In order of complexity, of the intellectual processes described, these categories are as follows:

1. Recall of specific facts;
2. Recognition of meaning or implication;
3. Selection of appropriate generalizations to explain phenomena;
4. Interpretation of data presented in a variety of forms,
5. Application of principles to solution of problems of a familiar type,
6. Analysis of unfamiliar constellations of events;
7. Evaluation of total situation;
8. Synthesis of data into new and meaningful wholes.

The results are shown in Table 2.5, where the categories refer to the above list.

Table 2.5. Classification of items from 10 biochemistry examinations in 1968

Paper	No. of items classified	Categories							
		1,	2,	3,	4,	5,	6,	7,	8,
A	8	8	3	2	—	1	—	2	1
B	8	8	8	2	—	1	—	3	1
C	9[a]	8	4	5	3	—	3	3	1
D	26	26	22	9	—	5	—	6	—
E	17[a]	17	2	8	—	2	—	—	—
F	9	7	6	2	—	—	—	4	—
G	16	16	16	2	—	—	—	—	—
H	14	14	3	—	—	—	—	—	3
I	23	19	3	17	—	—	1	17	2
J	26	12	10	4	1	1	4	23	1
Total:	364	135	89	51	4	10	8	58	9

[a] excluding M.C.q.s.

About 63 per cent of the questions were judged to fall into categories 1 and 2, and more often into these two together, than either of them alone. (It is possible to answer an essay question at one or several levels.) Many questions precluded answers at levels higher than 1 or 2, e.g. the majority of questions beginning with 'Describe . . .' or 'Outline . . .'. About 14 to 16 per cent respectively fell into categories 3 and 7, but two of the ten colleges were largely responsible for the latter. The remaining categories 4, 5, 6 and 8 were virtually unrepresented. It is true that categories 4 and 5 are said to be more commonly represented in practical examinations, but these are being phased out.

One department in a medical school has fundamentally reorganized its examination to achieve a variety of objectives, e.g.:

(i)   Multiple choice items are used to test recall of factual knowledge and familiar applications;

(ii)   Carefully designed questions including 'experimental data' are used to test the students' ability to account for results, to relate a solution to theoretical principles, and to suggest further experimental work;

(iii)   Ability to obtain and to synthesize information is tested by an essay for which six weeks preparation is allowed;

(iv)   Five traditional essay questions test students' ability to recall and to apply principles or to select generalizations.

Similar investigations into examinations in medicine[3] and physics[4] have shown similar emphasis on questions to which answers could be memorized and neglect of wider objectives.

Some teachers attempt to justify this by expressing concern that students should acquire a 'body of knowledge'. This has some considerable value if the inter-related concepts and patterns are learned which give structure to the subject; nevertheless, we question the adequacy of this objective alone.

David Warren Piper of the Unit devised a 7 x 6 array to help Mrs. D. Dallas of King's College, London, to organize her accumulation of objectives for the training of biology teachers. This was completed with the aid of a working party of biology tutors, but is to be revised.

The six main headings are as follows:
1.   Philosophy of the curriculum and role of the teacher;
2.   Content of courses taught;
3.   Classroom techniques;
4.   Integration of content and techniques;
5.   Organization and administration;
6.   Insight on own performance.

Each of these is considered from seven aspects, viz:
A.   Premises;
B.   Changes desired in attitudes and values;
C.   Knowledge to be gained;
D.   Skills required;
E.   Methods of teaching and learning situations;
F.   What should be assessed;
G.   Method of assessment.

For instance at the intersection of 2—content taught—and 1—premises—(i.e. 2A) we find—

(a)   a knowledge of primary education;
(b)   a need to accommodate a wide variety of degrees,
(c)   that students feel insecure outside their main subject area;
(d)   that students often unable to sort out basic concepts of science;
(e)   that students need to be willing to tackle all ability ranges, 11-18;
(f)   that students often have stereotype ideas of what constitutes good teaching method.

Each sub-category is further elaborated in the text which follows. Thus 2Ad reads: 'Students often emerge from university biology courses confused by a mass of particular evidence and quite devoid of a simple frame of reference on a variety of topics—this is particularly obvious in sixth form teaching, and if not dealt with in the initial training year it tends to produce a vicious circle. To expect them to sort out basic concepts without a tutor's help is unrealistic. Such work is also valuable for inservice updating for teachers.'

More than two hundred objectives in training biology teachers are specified and elaborated in this way; but despite their number, the initial matrix ensures their presentation in an easily comprehensible form. And, in common with most systematic schemes, changes are easily effected and their implications more readily understood than is the case when objectives remain subjective.

INTERMEDIATE AND SHORT TERM OBJECTIVES. FEEDBACK ON LEARNING

Statements of objectives have a number of advantages to students. The first is that intermediate goals are provided which give direction to the students' studies, thus increasing motivation. Too often students feel that they are faced with a mass of unrelated kinds of information to learn and fail to see a coherent design in their studies. If the scheme of objectives is available this problem is overcome. The second advantage is seen in the use of teaching techniques which state short term objectives and give immediate feedback on learning. Programmed texts, or tape/slide sequences accompanied by question books are typical examples. They serve a useful purpose in enabling students to catch up in areas of study they have missed, to work at their own pace through topics which they find difficult, or in revision. In every instance the student knows what is required of him and finds out almost immediately how success-ful his learning has been. Thus, stated objectives give direction and provide a form of continuous assessment simultaneously.

Although in the long run it is the teacher's aims and realistic methods of achieving these which are of paramount importance, short term objectives contribute to the students' confidence and help less able students to identify and overcome their diffi-culties.

Such short-term objectives are usefully stated in 'behavioural' terms—that is what the student will *do* when he is demonstrating that he has achieved the objective. I leave

Table 2.6. Assorted Objectives (from R. F. Mager, *Preparing Instructional Objectives,* Fearon, California, 1962, p. 55)

Are the objectives below stated in behavioural terms?	*Yes*	*No*
(*a*) To understand the principles of salesmanship		
(*b*) To be able to write three examples of the logical fallacy of the indistributed middle		
(*c*) To be able to understand the meaning of Ohm's Law		
(*d*) To be able to name the bones of the body		
(*e*) To be able to list the principles of secondary school administration		
(*f*) To know the plays of Shakespeare		
(*g*) To *really* understand the law of magnetism		
(*h*) To be able to identify instructional objectives that indicate what the learner will be doing when demonstrating achievement of the objective		

the interested reader with an exercise to complete. Consider whether the objectives in Table 2.6 name the act which the learner would be performing when demonstrating that he has achieved the objective. (Answers on p. 166).

References

1. P. J. Black, N. A. Dyson and D. A. O'Connor, *Phys. Educ.* **3**, 289 (1968).
2. R. M. Beard and K. Pole, *Brit. J. Med. Educ.* **5**, 13 (1971).
3. C. H. McGuire, *J. Med. Educ.* **38**, 556 (1963).
4. P. J. Black, *Phys. Educ.* **3**, 93 (1968).

CHAPTER 3

Classification of Educational Objectives

D. E. BILLING

Amongst teachers, it sometimes seems to be regarded as an impertinence to ask 'what are your goals?' or a question designed to elicit the same information, such as 'why are you teaching that?' Yet it is the students rather than ourselves who may not reach useful goals, and this hazard ought to make us think very carefully about our aims and objectives.

In fact, we are used to writing down learning goals for the student, except that we do it only in the form of examinations—by which stage the student can only perceive the purpose retrospectively. Mager suggests[1] that one way to get started on specifying objectives is 'to look over the examinations you use; they will tell you what you are using as standards of performance . . .'

To give the student a syllabus, in which a list of topics appears, is not very useful. This sort of document does not communicate the aims or approach or anything very important about the course to anyone—the external examiner or a new lecturer, for example. Thus, the syllabus entry 'Bragg's law' does not say anything very specific. However, if we examine the sort of assessment question set on Bragg's law, we may find that the student is required to give a diagram from which he can derive the law, and that he must be able to apply the equation to the interpretation of powder X-ray photographs. This information gives us the statement of objectives which are in fact being used. We are not saying that the examination determines the course, but that a survey of typical examination questions (each determined by the existing course) may enlighten us about our real goals. If the course is new, and there are no assessment questions to refer to, we may invent some to clarify the sort of thing which we expect the student to be able to do.

Objectives, therefore, need to specify what the student will be able to *do* at the completion of the course (or each stage of the course). Mager suggests[1] that useful objectives should specify the *behaviour* that the student will exhibit when attaining them, the *conditions* or *restrictions* under which he will work and the *criteria* of his success.

Blake[2] lists some purposes of specifying objectives as follows:

1.   To establish the behaviour desired of the student in precise terms, so that we know when to stop the teaching, i.e. when observable behaviour of the students and that specified in the objectives coincide;

2.   In conjunction with information about the students for whom the teaching is meant, to allow a preliminary selection of media to establish validity of teaching experience so that the students will perform properly on the real job for which they are training;

3.   When analysed into lower-level sub-objectives, to allow—
   (i)   pre-requisite abilities and knowledge to be defined;
   (ii) valid tests of these pre-requisites to be devised;
   (iii) valid tests of achievement of the objectives to be devised;
   (iv) appropriate teaching techniques to be chosen.

4.   When specified precisely in behavioural terms make it—
   (i)   easier for a student and/or teacher to decide whether he wishes to use the material constructed to achieve the objectives;
   (ii) possible to check and/or revise the quality of the lesson;
   (iii) impossible to criticize a lesson for *not* achieving objectives not specified.

In (3) above, it is suggested that objectives may be analysed into sub-objectives, and in doing so, we have introduced the idea of a hierarchy of objectives. Ways of deriving this hierarchy, in terms of what the learner must be able to do to achieve objectives at each level, have been suggested by Gagné[3] and by Mechner[4] (*see* Chap. 11). Thus, one of the broad aims of a course might be 'to enable students to appreciate the patterns and inter-relationships within scientific concepts'. One objective relating to this could be 'to develop an appreciation of the unifying nature of the concept of energy'. A relevant sub-objective would be 'the student will be able to give equations which show the involvement of the relevant form of energy in each type of physical interaction'. One such interaction might be the electrostatic force, and an appropriate sub-objective (at an even finer level of detail) would then be 'the student will be able to apply the expression for electrostatic potential to the solution of problems involving electrostatic forces'. At a still finer level we may have 'ability to manipulate simple algebraic equations' or we may decide that this is a pre-requisite ability.

In the example above, we have only indicated one of a large number of relevant objectives at each level. The decision as to relevance would need to take into account the other broad aims of the course. For example, if the course was for thirteen year old children, the emphasis on manipulating equations might be unfortunate. Similarly, if a broad aim were to develop critical thinking or creativity, the imposition of energy as a unifying concept might be too dogmatic.

In the example above, some of the objectives or sub-objectives describe the *behaviour* of the student when he is achieving them; these could easily be re-stated as assessment items—e.g. 'use the expression $V = e_1 e_2 / r$ to solve the following problem . . .' However, not all the goals are stated in behavioural terms—nor can they be so stated. Much of the present debate[5] over the desirability of behavioural objectives is not really a controversy about whether all objectives should be stated in terms of what the student will do, but about whether objectives which cannot be so stated are worth specifying. A reasonable solution to this problem would seem to be to write down all goals in whatever form first comes to mind, to further analyse them into a hierarchy, and then to attempt to write as many as possible in behavioural terms. Some order of priorities amongst the goals has then to be decided, but this should not overemphasize objectives which are behavioural.

In balancing aims against each other, it is necessary to consider their sources. The goal may be derived from the subject matter itself, from the needs of the individual student (emotional, physical, intellectual, material or aesthetic) and from social requirements (ethical, political and economic). The teachers and their institutions also determine aims for courses.

One way of classifying the levels of goals is in terms of long term (broad) aims and shorter term objectives. Scriven suggests[6] instead that there are three levels of learning 'outcomes', viz:

> (*a*)　The *conceptual* level which is relatively abstract (e.g. knowledge of patterns, understanding of applications of rules, attitude towards science);
> (*b*)　The *manifestational* level describes how the achievement of the objective may be demonstrated (e.g. discrimination between A and B, evaluation, problem-solving;
> (*c*)　The *operational* level specifies how the achievement of the objective is to be assessed (behavioural).

In designing a course, we hope to progress with increasing detail from the conceptual level, through the manifestational level to the operational level. Much of the treatment in Beard's paper has been at the conceptual level, and the rest of this chapter is devoted mainly to schemes of classification at the manifestational level. The operational level is covered in Chap. 16, where testing for attainment of objectives is treated. Much of the initiative for specifying objectives has in fact come from the field of achievement measurement.

SCHEMES FOR CLASSIFICATION

Objectives may involve the acquisition of abilities, aptitudes, attitudes, interests, motivation or personality traits etc. Those abilities associated with the manipulation and understanding of knowledge may be further classified.

A.　One commonly used list of abilities in this area (*the cognitive domain*) is due to Bloom[7] *et al.*:

1.　Knowledge
　　A.　Specifics
　　　　(i) Knowledge of terms
　　　　(ii) Knowledge of specific facts
　　B.　Knowledge of ways and means of dealing with specifics
　　　　(i) Conventions
　　　　(ii) Trends and sequences
　　　　(iii) Classification and categories
　　　　(iv) Criteria
　　　　(v) Methodology
　　C.　Knowledge of Universals and abstractions in a field
　　　　(i) Knowledge of principals and generalizations
　　　　(ii) Knowledge of theories and structures

2. Comprehension (grasping the meaning of material)
    A. Translation (converting from one form to another)
    B. Interpretation (explaining or summarizing material)
    C. Extrapolation (extending meaning beyond the data)

3. Application (using information in actual situations)

4. Analysis (breaking down information into its parts)
    A. Analysis of elements (identifying the parts)
    B. Analysis of relationships (identifying relationships)
    C. Analysis of organizational principles (identifying the way parts are organized).

5. Synthesis (putting parts together again)
    A. Production of a unique communication
    B. Production of a plan or proposed set of operations
    C. Derivation of a set of abstract relationships.

6. Evaluation (judging the value of a thing, for a given purpose, with given criteria)
    A. Judgements in terms of internal evidence
    B. Judgements in terms of external evidence

It is usually accepted that the difficulty of learning and of testing for these abilities increases from 'knowledge' to 'evaluation'. We may therefore call some objectives 'low-order' (e.g. knowledge), and others 'high-order' (e.g. evaluation). The best way to illustrate the meaning of Bloom's classification is to give examples of corresponding assessment items, some examples are given below:

Knowledge of Terminology

Which statement best defines 'heterogeneous'?

Knowledge of Specific Facts

What is the most important characteristic of a base?

Knowledge of Conventions

Which statement indicates correct usage of standard electrode potentials?

Knowledge of Trends and Sequences

What would be the shape of the curve for ionic radius versus atomic number?

Knowledge of Classifications

Which of the following is an example of an ionic hydride?

Knowledge of Criteria

What are the most important criteria for selecting orbitals which combine?

Knowledge of Methodology

What would be the best way to determine the structure of Ferrocene?

Knowledge of Principles and Generalizations

Which of the following principles is most useful in predicting shapes of molecules?

Knowledge of Theories and Structures

What evidence best supports the theory of crystal-field splitting?

    B.   Other abilities (e.g. the ability to work scientifically) involve attitudes as well as the learning and manipulation of concepts and facts. This area (*the 'affective domain'*) of value judgements, feelings, interests and motivation has been categorized by Krathwohl[8] *et al.*

1. Receiving (attending)
   A. Awareness (of stimuli, of aesthetic factors, of colour, form, arrangement);
   B. Willingness to receive (toleration of a stimulus, careful attendance when others speak, appreciation of alien cultural patterns, sensitivity to human needs);
   C. Controlled or selected attention (favoured stimulus selected despite distractions, alertness to human values, discriminations of mood and meaning of art).

2. Responding (active attention at low level, interests):
   A. Acquiescence in responding (compliance, passivity);
   B. Willingness to respond (capacity for voluntary activity, acceptance of responsibility);
   C. Satisfaction in response (emotional or pleasurable accompaniment to response).

3. Valuing (attitudes and beliefs):
   A. Acceptance of value (ascribing worth to events, behaviour, objects, beliefs, consistency);
   B. Preference for a value (seeking a value, examining all viewpoints);
   C. Commitment (certainty in beliefs, loyalty, advocacy).

4. Organization (of several relevant values):
   A. Conceptualization of a value (abstraction, relation to other values, exploration of characteristics of objects or values);
   B. Organization of a value system (ordered relationships between values).

5. Characterization by a value or value complex (generalization to control all one's behaviour, integration of beliefs, attitudes, ideas into total philosophy):
   A. Generalized set (internal consistency in system of values and attitudes);
   B. Characterization (philosophy of life of even greater inclusiveness covering all behaviour and knowledge).

Even if this scheme is accepted, it is rather difficult to see how it can be translated into assessment methods. Krathwohl does give examples, and some further examples are illustrated below:

Acceptance of a Value

Indicate your agreement or disagreement with the following statements, on a five-point scale from 1 (strongly disagree) to 5 (strongly agree):

The purpose of a scientific conference is generally to provide opportunities for —

(i) review of the state of the art;
(ii) presentation of current research findings,
(iii) solving problems;
(iv) consolidation of work in rapidly developing areas;
(v) understanding an unfamiliar area;
(vi) stimulating an interest;
(vii) informal discussions;
(viii) speeding up publication of results;
(ix) constructive criticism.

Preference for a Value

What type of the following conference activities would best fulfill each of the above functions:

A.   Invited Lectures;
B.   Presentation of submitted papers;
C.   Plenary discussion;
D.   Small-group discussions;
E.   Circulation of preprints;
F.   Formal social functions.

Satisfaction in Response

Indicate whether you do (S) or do not (D) get satisfaction from the activity mentioned in each item below. Indicate U if you are uncertain, or X if you have never performed the activity.

(*a*)   To experiment with plants to find out how various conditions of soil, water and light affect their growth;

(*b*)   To study rock formations and to learn how they developed,

(*c*)   To visit an observatory to learn how astronomers study the stars;

(*d*)   To read about how distances to inaccessible places are measured, such as from the earth to the sun, the height of a mountain etc.;

(*e*)   To read about new scientific developments.

(Objective: To measure interest in science in terms of pleasure in science activities.)

There is a tendency for scientists to leave these types of objectives to artists and sociologists, concentrating instead on the area of thinking rather than of believing. However, there are objectives of science courses which fall into the affective domain as illustrated by the search for truth, the preference for scientific methods of investigation, the advocacy of one theory against another, the recognition of significant results, and definition of acceptable limits of error, and the admiration for elegance. Krathwohl *et al.* have compared knowledge, analysis, synthesis and evaluation (cognitive realm) with receiving, conceptualization of a value, organization of a value system and characterization of a value system (affective area).

There is a third area, concerned with the development of muscular skills, manipulation and co-ordination of movements (*psychomotor domain*). Since chemistry is a practical science, it is necessary to attain many such skills as weighing, pipetting, glassblowing, filling a melting-point tube or centering a signal on a cathode ray tube. Training in and assessment of such skills may be rather haphazard at present, at least in institutions of higher education. Yet in industry, training is treated more seriously,[9] sometimes to the extent of applying skills analysis, task analysis or behavioural analysis methods. Since such skills are directly exhibited, when achieved, their testing does not usually present difficulties.

   C.   Simpson[10] has made an attempt to classify objectives in the psychomotor domain:

   1.   Perception
      1.1   Sensory stimulation (auditory, visual, tactile, taste, smell, kinesthetic), e.g. 'Awareness of difference in smell of various gases'.
      1.2   Cue selection (choosing stimuli relevant to the task), e.g. 'Recognition of operating difficulties with machinery through the sound of the machine'.
      1.3   Translation (deciding the action warranted by the selected stimuli), e.g. 'Ability to adjust the position of a specimen under a microscope'.

   2.   Set (readiness for action)
      2.1   Mental set, e.g. 'Knowledge of apparatus necessary to distil a liquid'.
      2.2   Physical set, e.g. 'Positioning of fingers preparatory to pipetting'.
      2.3   Emotional set, e.g. 'Desire to perform a dissection skillfully'.

   3.   Guided Response (performance of act under supervision)
      3.1   Imitation, e.g. 'Making up a nujol mull in the manner demonstrated'.
      3.2   Trial and Error, e.g. 'Discovering a suitable solvent for a compound'.

   4.   Mechanism (response is now habitual and part of a repertoire of possible responses to stimuli), e.g. 'Ability to connect up an oscilloscope'.

   5.   Complex overt response (high degree of skill with complex tasks)
      5.1   Resolution of uncertainty (no hesitation in performance), e.g. 'Skill in setting up and operating an NMR machine'.
      5.2   Automatic Performance (finely coordinated motor skill), e.g. 'Skill in glassblowing'.

   6.   Adapting and Originating—suggested as a possible additional category.

   D.   The three domains described by Bloom *et al.* may be grouped slightly differently in terms of 'knowledge', 'skills' and 'attitudes'. In this case, 'skills' span both the cognitive and psychomotor domains—e.g. problem-solving skills, glassblowing skills. Davidson has taken[11] this a stage further, dividing knowledge into 'factual' or 'conceptual' knowledge, attitudes into 'attitudes' or 'habits' and skills into 'motor', 'intellectual' or 'communication' skills. He also added the dimension of 'creativity', which otherwise is best accommodated under Bloom's cognitive 'synthesis' category.

   The simple division into 'knowledge', 'skills' and 'attitudes' has been accepted by Beard and is illustrated in her paper. On this basis, objectives are grouped into a column and appropriate learning activities and assessment methods listed in adjoining columns. Piper has suggested[12] the addition, to these tables, of a column headed 'premises'. This would list the assumptions being made when aims are suggested as important, or when certain teaching methods or assessment methods are linked to them. Such premises may form a useful point at which to begin a critical appraisal of a course design; they may therefore be seen as an even more fundamental stage than 'objectives'.

E.   Gagné considered[13] the stages through which the learner would pass in attaining concepts and in using them. The types of learning he classified in the following order of increasing sophistication:

> (i)   Signal learning;
> (ii)   Stimulus–Response learning;
> (iii)   Chaining;
> (iv)   Verbal association;
> (v)   Discrimination learning;
> (vi)   Concept learning;
> (vii)   Rule learning;
> (viii)   Problem solving.

Leith[14] proposes a similar scheme:

> (i)   Stimulus discrimination;
> (ii)   Response learning;
> (iii)   Response integration;
> (iv)   Association;
> (v)   Trial and Error learning;
> (vi)   Learning set formation;
> (vii)   Concept learning;
> (viii)   Concept integration;
> (ix)   Problem solving;
> (x)   Learning schemata.

F.   Ashford[15] used the following scheme, in designing College Chemistry Tests for the U.S. Armed Forces Institute:

I.   *Information*
Knowledge of important facts;
Knowledge of important terms;
Acquaintance with important concepts;
Verbal understanding of principles and theories;
General knowledge of the physical and chemical properties of substances.

II.   *Application of Principles*
Functional understanding of principles and theories of chemistry and their inter-relationships;
Application of a definition;
Application of principles in new situations taken from everyday life;
Interpretation of a set of data and drawing conclusions from them.

III.   *Quantitative Application of Principles*
For example:
Calculations involving gas laws;
Calculations involving molecular weights;
Balancing equations.

IV.   *The Scientific Method*
Relation between theory and experiment;
Assumption necessary for a given conclusion;

Determining whether a statement is true in terms of observations, theories or definitions;
Factors which should be controlled in an experiment.

Gowenloch *et al.*[16] modified this scheme, also for the purpose of constructing chemistry tests:

A. *Knowledge*
The ability to recall information such as—
 (*a*)   the chemical and physical properties of the more important elements and their compounds;
 (*b*)   definitions of important chemical terms;
 (*c*)   important chemical conventions and concepts;
 (*d*)   the theories of chemistry.

B. *Application*
The ability to apply factual information, principles or theories—
 (*a*)   to a described situation which is familiar (in the textbook or laboratory sense) and in which the principle to be applied is clearly indicated;
 (*b*)   to a prescribed situation which is not familiar and the principle to be applied is not immediately obvious;
 (*c*)   in the interpretation of supplied data;
 (*d*)   to the solution of quantitative problems.

C. *Scientific Method*
The ability to—
 (*a*)   relate theoretical ideas to experimental results, i.e. to explain phenomena in terms of theory;
 (*b*)   determine what assumptions are inherent in conclusions drawn from experimental evidence;
 (*c*)   select the correct apparatus (modifying it if required) for any particular programme of experimental procedures, and to realize the possible dangers of misuse;
 (*d*)   make observations (such as burette readings) rejecting the obviously wrong and processing the remainder, realizing that the most accurate experimental result is determined by the least accurate observation;
 (*e*)   devise experimental processes (i) to test a theoretical explanation of observed phenomena or (ii) to select the correct explanation from a series of possible explanations.

 G.   Many aims of courses might be linked to the uses of science in industry, and the relevance to society. Bennett[17] considers the training which a graduate must undergo on entering the chemical industry. He sets out the goals of this training in terms of a Job Specification for an applied research chemist:

Main Duties

A. *Prescribed*
 1.   To work towards specific research objectives allocated to him by his superior;
 2.   To write the corresponding research programmes, detailing the broad lines to be followed;
 3.   To forecast the time they will take and the resources required;
 4.   To be familiar with any process, test or procedure carried out in his section in connection with the programme;

5.   To use such techniques as are available (statistical, mathematical, chemical or mechanical) to achieve the research objectives with the minimum expenditure and effort;

6.   To assign a selected proportion of the work to his subordinates, to supervise and assess their work and to be responsible for effective employment;

7.   To be responsible for their safety and on-the-job training and to suggest suitable off-the-job training and further education;

8.   To motivate his subordinates by example and attitude, by consulting them and keeping them fully informed on relevant aspects of the work;

9.   To ensure the accurate recording of all experimental data, conclusions and hypotheses in the appropriate form;

10.   To communicate the progress and results of his work, and its significance, to his supervisor and to other staff through reports and meetings, as the job objective requires;

11.   To assist other staff in the pursuit of their objectives, as necessary;

12.   To improve his own knowledge and expertise in appropriate areas of information and technique;

13.   To consider the significance of each duty performed, and to allocate priorities between them, in relation to the objective of the job.

B.   *Discretionary*

1.   To arrange and supervise plant trials;

2.   Within his job objective, to develop the product or process as he sees best;

3.   To consult with other staff as he wishes;

4.   To follow up speculative leads that may emerge and be relevant to the job objective, keeping his supervisor informed.

These duties will require certain knowledge, skills and attitudes, and Bennett goes on to give appropriate examples, along with a list of specific points to be covered during the training programme.

Knowledge, Skills and Attitudes for an Applied Research Chemist (extract from Bennett[17])

(Degree of attainment: A = application; P = practioner; E = expert)

KNOWLEDGE	SKILL	ATTITUDE
To appreciate a problem and select lines for research		
1. Company and departmental objectives (E)	1. To define problems (E)	A critical enquiry and inventive frame of mind
2. Knowledge equivalent to a science degree (P)	2-3. To postulate possible routes to a solution (E)	
3. Relevant technology		

To organize the work

1. Raw materials (E)	1-3. Process equipment, operating and laboratory techniques needed for the work (P)	A determination to be professionally competent
2. Processes (E)		
3. Products (E)		
4. Hazards and safety regulations (E)	4. To handle any chemical or equipment safely (E)	
5. State of relevant present knowledge in science and technology (E)	5. To use all sources of information (library, filing systems etc.) (P)	
6. Patent position (A)		
7. Methods of planning research (P)	7. (*a*) Problem analysis (E) (*b*) Critical examination technique (P) (*c*) Critical path scheduling (P)	A systematic, purposeful approach to work
8. Mathematical, statistical, chemical and physical techniques available (A)	8. Use of relevant techniques, including calculating machines and computers (A/P)	Cost consciousness
9. Cost of materials, equipment and services (A)		
10. Requisitioning procedures (A)		

Industry needs graduates with such abilities, and vocational courses in higher education should derive their aims from such needs. This question is explored more fully in Chap. 4.

H.   Other lists of objectives have been prepared by the various Nuffield groups,[18] by the Science Masters' Association,[19] the American Council on Education,[20] Nedelsky,[21] Frutchley & Tyler,[22] Zyve,[23] and many others.[24] These schemes have been reviewed by Lewis,[25] by the Schools Council[26] and by Wheeler.[27] Thomson[28] carried out a survey of opinion about aims of secondary school chemistry courses in seven European countries.

I.   The description of a student's personality may also be an objective, since it affects the suitability of types of teaching method,[29] and also job-satisfaction and therefore career decision. Much work has been done in measuring the personality factors of creative scientists.[30] One well known categorization of this area is Cattell's Scheme of sixteen personality factors.[31]

J. Torrance,[32] in connection with studies of creativity has suggested that the aims of courses should emphasize *thinking* rather than *learning.* He classifies objectives according to the types of mental operation in which students must engage: Cognition, Memory, Convergent Behaviour, Divergent Thinking, Evaluation. There are clearly relationships here with Bloom's categories. Convergent abilities are often classified in a hierarchy of general, group and specific intellectual skills,[33] and measured by means of intelligence tests[34] or tests of reasoning power.[35] Tests of divergent abilities (creativity) are not so well developed.[32,36]

SELECTION OF OBJECTIVES

A number of very difficult decisions must be made when selecting those aims which will be emphasized in a course. No generally accepted criteria for selection exist. Unless these problems can be solved, intuitive ways of course design will continue to be the norm. It is tempting to suggest that large numbers of courses, each emphasizing particular sorts of goals, should be available for the students to choose. This would avoid the balancing of priorities of vocational aims and liberal educational aims against each other in the same course. Such a situation would not preserve the student's career options; some appropriate courses are described in the chapters by Roberts and Ronayne.

A possible way of avoiding the conflict of liberal and vocational goals, is hinted at in Hirst's views[37] about liberal education. Liberal education is equated with the pursuit of knowledge, and the forms of knowledge determine the curriculum. However, Hirst is more interested in the *method* of (say) science and its *criteria* for success than in factual knowledge. In this sense, a liberal science course would not consist in a superficial coverage of scientific facts, but in actually *doing* science in order to become familiar with devising and testing hypotheses. Breadth would be achieved by studying in *depth* a carefully selected number of paradigm examples. The depth of study might entail Epstein's research paper approach,[38] Harding's notional experiments[39] and projects possibly as extensive as those described in the chapter by Eaborn. The activity of designing and performing real scientific investigations may then be seen as a link between liberal and vocational types of course. Jevons suggests that another approach is to study the literature, either centralizing the course around a reading list, or using Conant's case history method.[40]

References

1. R. F. Mager, *Preparing Instructional Objectives,* Fearon, California 1962.
2. C. Blake, unpublished report, 1971.
3. R. M. Gagné, in *Teaching Machines and Programmed Learning,* Vol. 2, R. Glaser (Ed.), National Education Association, U.S.A. 1965, p. 21.
4. F. Mechner, in *Teaching Machines and Programmed Learning,* Vol. 2, R. Glaser (Ed.), National Education Association, U.S.A. 1965, p. 441.
5. P. E. Roscove, *Educ. Technol.* **11,** 36 (1971); J. M. Muchmore, *Educ. Technol.* **11,** 45 (1971).
6. M. Scriven, in *Perspectives of Curriculum Evaluation,* R. Stake (Ed.), Rand-McNally, Chicago 1967.

7. B. S. Bloom (Ed.), *Taxonomy of Educational Objectives: The Cognitive Domain,* McKay, New York 1956.
8. D. R. Krathwohl, B. S. Bloom and B. B. Masia, *Taxonomy of Educational Objectives Handbook II: Affective Domain,* McKay, New York 1964.
9. T. H. Boydell, *BACIE Journal* **25**, 53 (1971); A. J. Romiszowski (Ed.), *The Systems Approach to Education and Training,* Kogan Page, London 1970.
10. E. Simpson, in *Behavioural Objectives in Curriculum Development,* M. B. Kapfer (Ed.), Educational Technology, New York 1970.
11. J. M. C. Davidson, unpublished notes on systems analysis in education, 1971.
12. D. W. Piper, personal communication, 1971.
13. R. M. Gagné, *The Conditions of Learning,* Rinehart & Winston, New York 1965.
14. G. O. M. Leith, *Brit. J. Educ. Technol.* **1**, 116 (1969).
15. T. A. Ashford, *J. Chem. Educ.* **21**, 386 (1944).
16. B. G. Gowenlock, D. M. McIntosh and A. W. Mackaill, *Chem. Brit.* **6**, 341 (1970).
17. P. Bennett, *Chem. Brit.* **6**, 482 (1970).
18. *Nuffield Foundation Science Teaching Project, Chemistry: Introduction and Guide,* Longmans/Penguin, London 1966; Science 5-13 Project, *With Objectives in Mind,* MacDonald, London 1971.
19. Science Masters' Association, *The Teaching of General Science Pt. II,* Murray, London 1938; *Science and Education, A Policy Statement,* Murray, London 1961.
20. P. L. Dressel and L. B. Mayhew, in *General Education: Explorations in Evaluation,* Council on Education, New York 1954.
21. L. Nedelsky, *Science Teaching and Testing,* Harcourt, Brace & World, New York 1965.
22. F. P. Frutchley and R. W. Taylor, in *The Construction and Use of Achievement Examinations,* H. E. Hawkes, E. F. Lindquist and C. R. Mann (Eds.), Harrap, London 1937.
23. D. L. Zyve, *J. Educ. Psychol.* **18**, 525 (1927).
24. V. H. Noll, *Teachers Coll. Record* **35**, 1 (1933); O. Kesslar, *Sci. Educ.* **29**, 273 (1945); L. M. Heil, P. E. Kambly, M. Mainarde and L. Weisman, in *The Forty-Fifth Yearbook of the National Society for the Study of Education,* N. B. Henry (Ed.), University of Chicago 1946; M. A. Burmester, *Sci. Educ.* **36**, 259 (1952); G. M. Dunning, *Sci. Educ.* **38**, 191 (1954).
25. D. G. Lewis, *Educ. Res.* **7**, 186 (1964).
26. *Changes in School Science Teaching, Schools Council Curriculum Bulletin No. 3,* Evans/Methuen Education, London 1970.
27. D. K. Wheeler, *Curriculum Process,* University of London Press 1967.
28. J. J. Thompson, *Educ. Chem.* **8**, 170 (1971).
29. G. O. M. Leith, *Educ. Res.* **11**, 193 (1969).
30. R. B. Cattell and H. J. Butcher, *Prediction of Achievement and Creativity,* Bobbs-Merrill, New York 1968; F. Barron and C. W. Taylor (Eds.), *Scientific Creativity,* Wiley, New York 1963; F. E. Jones, *J. Appl. Psychol.* **48**, 134 (1964); J. A. Chambers, *Psychol. Monographs* **78**, No. 7 (1964).
31. R. B. Cattell, *The Scientific Analysis of Personality,* Penguin, London 1965; R. B. Cattell and H. W. Eber, *Handbook for the Sixteen Personality Factor Questionnaire,* Champaign, Illinois 1968.
32. E. P. Torrance, *Education and the Creative Potential,* University of Minnesota Press 1963.
33. C. Burt, *Brit. J. Educ. Psychol.* **9**, 45 (1939); *Brit. J. Statist. Psychol.* **3**, 40 (1950).
34. P. E. Vernon, *Intelligence and Attainment Tests,* University of London Press, London 1960.
35. C. W. Valentine, *Reasoning Tests,* Oliver & Boyd, London 1954.
36. L. Hudson, *Contrary Imaginations,* Penguin, London 1967; *Frames of Mind,* Penguin, London 1970.

37. P. H. Hirst, in *Philosophical Analysis and Education,* R. D. Archamboult (Ed.), Routledge & Kegan Paul, London 1965.
38. H. T. Epstein, *Strategy for Education,* Oxford University Press, Oxford 1970.
39. A. G. Harding, *Project Work—To Measure or to Learn?* Conference on Modern Methods in Teaching Science, Liverpool Polytechnic 1972.
40. F. R. Jevons, *The Teaching of Science,* Allen & Unwin, London 1970.

CHAPTER 4

Tertiary Science Courses in Relation to the Needs of Industry

D. T. L. JONES

THE ROLE OF TERTIARY SCIENCE COURSES

In his book *Technology and the Academics,* Sir Eric Ashby describes[1] the 'split personality' in the universities which results from a conflict between those who see their function as being to 'give undivided loyalty to the kingdom of the mind' and those 'for whom the university is an institution with urgent and essential obligations to modern society'.

In later years this kind of group schizophrenia was recognized as a one-sided disorder, for example, by the Committee under Prof. Swann in its report on studies of the flow into employment of scientists, engineers and technologists. The report expressed[2] considerable concern about the nature of scientific education and, in particular, observed that 'It is of great importance to change a widespread belief that academic research is the only respectable outcome of a scientific education.' Indeed they describe one of the requirements of a course as being to 'produce persons of high ability who are willing to apply their talents in industry and schools and not, as at present, almost exclusively in higher education and pure research.'

This distinction, between the apparent aims of many of those concerned with undergraduate education and the needs of society, encouraged the development of new degree courses sponsored by a Council for National Academic Awards and generally located in establishments of Further Education which have an historical allegiance to vocational objectives. The Robbins Committee in proposing the formation of the C.N.A.A. indicated[3] that the degrees 'should give new impetus to the development of vocational higher education in Great Britain and, in particular, should remedy weaknesses in the nature and organization of technological education and research.'

In considering tertiary science courses in relation to the needs of industry, one recognizes that two paths are open to the designer and teacher of these courses. He either admits to a lack of concern for the vocational destiny of his students and regards his educational provision as an end in itself, or he at least considers the suitability of his educational provision as a preparation for employment. In either case, he must be aware that the great majority of students on a tertiary science course are there because they want to become professional scientists.

The academic scientist should also dwell on the words of Lord Bowden[4] who said 'I think the world has become sceptical of the claims and pretensions of science and of engineering because so many academic scientists and engineers have detached themselves from the harsh world in which we all have to live and have had very little to do with some of the vitally important problems which confront ordinary citizens.'

PRESENT AND FUTURE EMPLOYMENT PATTERNS

As a first step in concerning ourselves with the future of our students we must try and establish their likely employment outlets.

The following approximate data[5] for 1970 show that about 60 per cent of the active stock (totalling 160,000) of qualified scientists in Great Britain were employed in industry and commerce.

Applied research and development in industry	30%
Marketing, education, training, management, planning and other non-research and development work in industry and commerce	30%
Schools and further education (including polytechnics)	20%
Government organizations, research associations, nationalized industries, etc.	10%
Universities	10%

Of those in industry at any one time, about 50 per cent work in areas other than research and development and a large proportion of those in research and development will at some later stage transfer to some other area of activity. It has been estimated that only 15 per cent of scientists in industry spend their whole career in the R & D field.

Our concern however is with the likely employment picture in the future, and forecasts of demand for qualified manpower are notoriously hazardous. It seems to be certain that many newly qualified chemists in future cannot be employed as chemists, if the present trend in the rate of their production continues. Some fields will be regularly saturated. It has been calculated that, after the recent expansion in the universities, the yearly need for university chemistry staff will be about thirty.[6] It also looks as if the employment picture for industrial R & D chemists has reached some sort of plateau.

There is little doubt that more and more of our science graduates will need to take up employment in areas not directly related to laboratory science. This trend is already apparent; the proportion of qualified scientists in the manufacturing industries who were employed in research and development fell from 55 per cent in 1962 to 49·9 per cent in 1968.[5]

AIMS OF COURSES

Now, in defining the objectives for vocational higher education courses, it is clearly important to keep at least the present employment picture in mind, while watching for detectable trends in changes of employment. This is especially important if we assume that a different educational preparation at degree level is required for the prospective research and development worker compared with the prospective non-R & D scientist; and this is open to debate.

In any case, an undergraduate course which confines itself to academic scientific considerations and which has an implied, if not declared, major objective of the preparation of students for a research role (whether academic or applied), shows a lack of concern for their future.

The present employment situation, together with uncertainties about the future, suggests that a major overall objective even though a somewhat vague one, is to prepare students for flexibility in their future employment.

To establish more detailed objectives, one needs to investigate the requirements of various occupations which attract science graduates. Since the majority of graduates are likely to find employment in industry, the following areas of information are particularly relevant:

(*a*)   The views of industrial scientists concerning the abilities, attributes and attitudes best suited to a career in industry.

(*b*)   The views of industrial scientists with respect to their own educational upbringing and their views about possible improvements in course design.

Surveys of such views[7,8,9] have recently been carried out by several agencies, and we turn now to some of the results reported.

'INDUSTRY, SCIENCE AND UNIVERSITIES' (Docksey report, 1970)[7]

A working party of the universities and industry joint committee studied a sample of companies which together employ 59 per cent of all the qualified scientists in industry. They found that only 4 per cent of industries recruit staff for complete careers in R & D, the remainder expecting or providing for transfer into other areas after an initial spell in R & D; and 13 per cent of the senior managers in the companies are qualified scientists.

Seventy-nine per cent of the companies said that they could not recruit all the qualified scientists, engineers and technologists of the right quality and in the right discipline to meet current and anticipated needs. Reasons given for this dissatisfaction with graduate recruitment were that a high proportion of top class graduates are retained by universities, that industry has a poor image amongst science graduates, and that graduates are wanting in quality because university courses are inadequate. Views about the inadequacies of graduate potential are shown in Table 4.1.

Sandwich course students were thought to be better with respect to commercial attitudes by 24 per cent of the companies.

In considering the design of courses, the extent to which specialist training should be included brought a wide range of views. At the extremes, 23 per cent said that one-fifth or less of an undergraduate course should be specialist training, while

10 per cent said that four-fifths or more should be specialist. Opinions about those aspects which should be taught at university are shown in Table 4.2.

Other skills which were suggested for inclusion in university courses are: economics, presentation of scientific and technical information, personnel management, mathematics, statistics or computer technology. The importance of fundamental knowledge was emphasized, together with the applications of knowledge.

Table 4.1. (From Docksey report[7])

| | Views that the potential of graduate scientists: | | |
	is adequate %	is not adequate %	seriously limits usefulness %
Ability to think into problems especially outside specific qualifications	46	50	4
Ability to express themselves in writing	31	61	8
Ability to express themselves orally and to instruct others	44	53	3
Aptitude for commercial thinking	16	57	27

Table 4.2. (From Docksey report[7])

| | Graduates potential in applying these skills is: | | | |
	Should be taught %	good %	fair %	poor %
Methods and techniques of research	82	22	67	11
Problem solving as members of a team	67	19	69	12
Understanding of technological economics	80	5	27	68

'RELATIONSHIP BETWEEN UNIVERSITY COURSES IN CHEMISTRY AND THE NEEDS OF INDUSTRY' (Eaborn report, 1970)[8]

A joint committee of the Royal Society and the Royal Institute of Chemistry studied questionnaires returned by random samples of 440 undergraduates, 329 post-graduate students, 417 university teaching staff, 352 recent graduates in industry and 250 senior industrialists, all of whom were chemists.

Both undergraduates (72%) and recent graduates (60%) were mainly of the view that there was too much learning of facts required in the courses they experienced. In addition, many undergraduates thought that their course was biased towards fields in which teaching staff were interested (65%), but disagreed with the suggestion that their course was too easy (66%) or that it demanded the same intellectual approach as the sixth form work (63%). The majority of recent graduates felt that more tutorials and/or seminars were necessary (67%), and that their course had been a poor preparation for a career as an administrator in industry (63%). Nevertheless the largest number of them expected (39%) and wanted (38%) to be working mainly in administration in 15 years' time, whereas only 15 per cent expected and 14 per cent wanted to be working mainly in research after the same period.

Commercial subjects such as industrial management, sociology and economics were found to be relevant to their career by 69 per cent of recent graduates. Only 29 per cent of them encountered these subjects at undergraduate level, although 57 per cent would have liked to have studied them on their undergraduate course and 82 per cent of the post-graduate level. Report writing was considered to be relevant to the careers of 84 per cent of the recent graduates. This was studied by 17 per cent of them, and 34 per cent would have liked to have studied the subject on their undergraduate course. Other subjects thought to be desirable for undergraduate and postgraduate studies included technological subjects (37%, 30%) such as chemical engineering and fuels, matrix methods (37%, 58%) such as operational research, critical path analysis and linear programming, and computer science (38%, 46%).

The usefulness of sandwich courses was indicated by recent graduates (mean = 2·0 on a scale from very useful = 1 to not useful at all = 5), and those who did sandwich courses expressed their usefulness in making an informed career decision (2·1) and the extent to which they gained an advantage over colleagues who did non-sandwich courses (2·2).

The sample of senior industrialists were asked about the extent to which they agreed with various statements applied to first degree chemistry courses. The important results are shown in Table 4.3 for non-sandwich and sandwich (in brackets)

Table 4.3. Senior Industrialists' Views on Non-sandwich and (Sandwich) Courses. (From Eaborn report[8])

	Tend to agree %	Tend to disagree %
Good coverage of commercial subjects, e.g. industrial management, economics, sociology	0 (13)	92 (58)
Gives students insight into the problems of industry	4 (82)	89 (4)
Good training in report writing, use of English	9 (14)	77 (60)
Provides a chemist who is immediately useful to industry	7 (69)	72 (9)
Not orientated to chemists going into industry	72 (10)	12 (76)
Indication of ability to work at management level	6 (4)	74 (70)
Only a guarantee of knowledge, not how to apply it	70 (30)	11 (37)

courses. Table 4.4 lists in rank-orders those qualities felt to be necessary for chemists working in industry by more than 50 per cent of the senior industrialists.

Senior industrialists indicated the qualifications required for positions in their

Table 4.4. Qualities Necessary for a Chemist Working in Industry. (From Eaborn report[8])

For R & D	%	For administration, sales, etc.	%
Drive and enthusiasm	73	Drive and enthusiasm	69
Capacity for original thought	72	Ability to get on with people	66
Capacity for logical and analytical		Personal qualities are more important	
argument	70	than above average scientific ability	59
Ability to work as part of team	65	Willingness and apparent ability	
Flexibility of outlook	63	to assume responsibility	59
Ability to get on with people	58	Flexibility of outlook	58
Ability to get on with research by		Ambition and initiative	58
themselves	52	Ability to work as part of team	57
Imagination	52	Organizing ability	56
Ambition and initiative	51	A broad general education	51

company; in selecting from applicants for research positions, only 8 per cent stated that a Ph.D is necessary, a good first degree being sufficient for 71 per cent of the sample.

'THE EDUCATION OF SCIENTISTS FOR INDUSTRY' (Jones, 1969)[9]

This study involved an analysis of questionnaires returned by 1400 members of the Royal Institute of Chemistry and the Institute of Physics. The extent to which various subjects or techniques were thought to be useful in the light of industrial experience is shown in Table 4.5, together with an indication of the percentage of the sample who received instruction in the same topics during their academic training.

In suggesting other useful topics, respondents made much mention of management and organization topics such as management theory, economics, marketing, project evaluation and decision-making. A considerable number also mentioned topics concerned with human relations, such as personnel management, psychology, and co-operation and communications with non-scientists.

Respondents were asked to select, from a given list of attributes those which they thought to be particularly desirable in scientists occupying four different managerial positions in industry. The results are shown in Table 4.6, and over 50 per cent indicated that important attributes for all four positions are: ability to communicate, ability to get on with people, ability to delegate authority, desire to accept responsibility and professional integrity. Other suggestions of important attributes fall into two groups:

(*a*)   A creative, inventive ability; an enquiring mind open to new ideas; an analytical logical approach; a sound fundamental knowledge of the subject; an ability for hard work.

(*b*)   An ability to inspire others and command respect, an understanding of human relations; sensitivity to other people's feelings, especially with respect to subordinates.

In considering the degree of importance of certain attitudes for an industrial scientist, the majority of the sample of chemists indicated that the following are important or extremely important: identification with company success (79%); concern for the necessity of budgeting and cost saving (79%); belief in the profit

Table 4.5. Percentages of Scientists who Consider Various Topics to be Useful, and Percentages who Received Instruction in them. (From Jones[9])

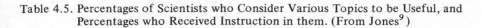

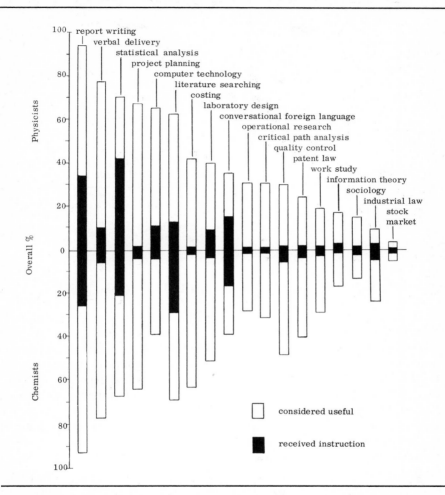

motive (59%); appreciation of the importance of the selling function (70%); acceptance of management decisions (67%).

The chemists indicated that the following parts of undergraduate courses could be reduced to make way for new topics (in decreasing order of frequency of mention):

(*a*) 'Cookery book', classical, repetitive practical activity;

(*b*) Specialist 'frontiers of knowledge', speculative, highly theoretical material;

(*c*) Factual, memory exercising, parrot learning textbook material;

(*d*) Classical, historical interest, obsolete outmoded material.

The main suggestions for course design, to improve the preparation of students for industry were (in decreasing order of frequency):

(*a*) Get students into industry for a period of their undergraduate training;

(*b*) Project work, both by individuals and teams, to replace many of the set experiments. Projects should make use of modern instrumental techniques, and in

Table 4.6. Scientists' Views on the Relative Importance of Various Attributes for Scientists Occupying Different Positions. (From Jones[9])

Percentage responses of whole sample

	Plant Manager	Research Group Leader	Technical Service Manager	Marketing or Planning Manager
100				
		← communicate		
90	← communicate		← communicate	← communicate
	← delegate			
		← integrity	← with people	
80	← with people	← critical		← with people
	← command			
	← responsibility			
		← memory		
		← team spirit		
70		← with people		
	← down to earth	← delegate		
		← tenacity		
			← integrity	← appearance
60			← responsibility	← responsibility
	← integrity	← responsibility	← delegate	← delegate
			← down to earth	← integrity
50			← appearance	
			← memory	← ambition
	← team spirit			← critical
				← down to earth
40	← critical		← critical	← tenacity
	← tenacity			
			← tenacity	
	← ambition	← command	← team spirit	← team spirit
30		← ambition	← command	← command
	← appearance	← down to earth	← ambition	
		← manual		
20	← manual		← manual	← memory
		← appearance		
	← memory			
10				
				← manual
0				

Description of attributes—ability to *communicate*; *down to earth* attitude; ability to get on *with people*; ability to *delegate* authority; *tenacity*; personal *appearance*; *critical* attitude; power of *command*; *ambition*; desire to accept *responsibility*; *team spirit*; *manual* dexterity; professional *integrity*; *memory* for scientific information.

some cases be concerned with real industrial problems, and should involve considerations such as costing, planning and construction and others important in industry;

(*c*)   Greater emphasis on applications of science to industry. Undergraduate courses should seek to remedy the poor image of industrial science;

(*d*)   Greater contact between academics and industrialists. Industrialists should participate in lectures, tutorials and project activities, while academics should engage in joint applied research projects with industry;

(*e*)   Emphasis should be placed on basic theory and fundamentals rather than complex treatments. Specialization should be reserved for post-graduate attention;

(*f*)   Lectures dealing with the structure and aims of industry, the role of the industrial scientist, industrial relations and the relative functions of different industrial departments;

(*g*)   Lectures on management techniques, business studies and the economic implications of industrial activity;

(*h*)   Special training in report writing and public speaking. Development of communication abilities both with writing and speaking.

DISCUSSION

The various surveys show that, as well as such obvious matters as a sound basic scientific education and a grasp of certain areas of mathematics, there are clearly several objectives which demand attention regardless of the vocational future of the students. These areas are neglected in most undergraduate courses at present, but are especially important in view of the need for flexibility in future employment.

1.   There is universal agreement about the ignorance of science undergraduates with respect to the role of the scientist in industry, the nature and structure of industry and the applications of science to industry. This lack is not only a serious one with respect to vocational misguidance, as we have already seen, but seems to me to be indefensible if we are to produce a well educated scientist in our present technologically based society.

The impact of science on society, with respect to the quality of life, the destiny of man, and the growing insistence that scientists be more concerned with their social responsibilities suggests that the science and industry objective be extended to encompass science and the whole of society.

2.   Another shortcoming of scientists, which seems to be universally recognized, is their limitation in the communications field—including both the ability at written and spoken communication. I would not suggest that we necessarily provide formal lessons in grammar and speech training—my concern here is with defining objectives, and not means.

3.   A recurring theme which runs through various described requirements for a modern scientist is a need for him to work well in a team situation. He needs to understand the problems of team work, human relations and industrial psychology. This seems to me to be such an important requirement that an objective of a course should include some sort of preparation for the team situation.

4.   There is a need for students of science to be able to exercise their creative inclinations with respect to their studies. We immediately think of project work and would want to involve a student in situations in which he would be likely to find himself in employment. These activities would require him to consider matters such as the economic factors and planning techniques associated with industrial practices, so that he can better appreciate the inter-relationships between different industrial functions.

CONCLUSION

The intention here is not to suggest that the wishes of industrial scientists should be strictly adhered to, in designing an undergraduate course for prospective industrial scientists. If, however, we regard specialist science courses as professional ones (in the same way as courses in medicine, engineering and architecture), rather than solely as an intellectual enterprise (in the manner of undergraduate courses in history, English and philosophy), then we should attend very carefully to the views of professional scientists.

A concern for the vocational future of our students requires that we do far more than fill them with science. The results of the surveys present[7,8,9] many ways of achieving the objectives that are thought to be desirable. However, the most valuable resource in education continues to be the human one, and the variety of human resources denies a uniquely right way of reaching an educational objective. Different methods are best suited to different individuals or teams.

I would like to conclude with a quotation from a UNESCO conference on Education in a Technological Society:[10] 'The tendency of the intellectual to create men in his own image is strong. It is also dangerous. If a country, by conferring prestige, amenities and security upon an academic type of training, sets out to produce in mass the man who never takes his coat off, it will have served its people ill.'

References

1. E. Ashby, *Technology and the Academics,* Macmillan, London 1958.
2. *Interim Report of the Working Group on Manpower Parameters for Scientific Growth,* H.M.S.O., London 1966.
3. *Higher Education: Report of the Committee under the Chairmanship of Lord Robbins,* H.M.S.O., London 1963.
4. Lord Bowden, 'Science in Crisis', *New Scientist,* 21 January 1971.
5. Department of Trade and Industry, *Persons with Qualifications in Engineering, Technology and Science,* H.M.S.O., London 1970.
6. D. Davies and E. Stern, *Pure Appl. Chem.* 22, 177 (1970).
7. Industry, Science and Universities, Report of the UIJC Confederation of British Industry, London 1970.
8. *Report of the Committee of Enquiry into the Relationship between University Courses in Chemistry and the Needs of Industry,* Royal Institute of Chemistry, London 1970.
9. D. T. L. Jones, *The Education of Scientists for Industry,* Society for Research into Higher Education, London 1969.
10. *Education in a Technological Society,* UNESCO, Paris 1952.

II. CURRICULUM DEVELOPMENTS

CHAPTER 5

Curriculum Development in Tertiary Chemistry Courses

A. K. HOLLIDAY

My aim is, first, to look at some factors that have influenced the development of our present chemistry curricula, and then to examine the factors which must, I believe, influence future developments.

Up to the present day, chemistry courses at both the secondary and tertiary levels have been dominated by two principal requirements—the need to produce chemists for industry and the need to nourish research in both universities and industry. These essentially utilitarian requirements can be traced back to the German schools of chemistry which have greatly influenced modes of thought about chemistry teaching here and in the United States. We need not pursue the historical background any further; but we must note that these requirements have, until recently, strongly influenced school as well as tertiary curricula, and that some consequences of these requirements are so familiar to us that we take them for granted. Let us then look at some of these consequences; I select four of particular importance:

1. Chemistry courses must provide a comprehensive coverage of the whole subject.

2. Chemistry at school must provide a foundation for tertiary chemistry, i.e. a certain body of knowledge must be assumed as the starting point for tertiary chemistry education.

3. Chemistry courses must always be practical.

4. Chemistry courses must train people for research and at the same time make them suitable for employment *as chemists* in industry, in teaching and elsewhere.

The need for comprehensive coverage has meant that chemistry curricula have always been designed with the primary aim of achieving an adequate *content*. Most of us who teach chemistry at tertiary level tend to be obsessed with the idea that a student 'must know something about . . .' It is conceivable that chemistry curricula were, decades ago, comprehensive in their coverage; it is manifestly absurd to suppose that they are so now. But because of the preoccupation with content, school chemistry curricula, dominated by G.C.E. syllabuses, have, until recently, been almost exclusively designed for those going further in chemistry, so that the tertiary teacher could assume that some of his work in covering chemistry as a whole had already been done for him at school.

After several years at school and three or four years of tertiary education, the aspiring research chemist of today is still not considered to know enough, and his course work is now often extended into the postgraduate period; Ph.D. students are expected to attend courses (which they see as only marginally relevant to their research interests) and to face examinations set on such courses. So we produce young chemists, who have spent a decade or so in learning about chemistry. *Surely* they *must* be well-equipped for any job? Not so; they are sometimes told that they are too specialized and too narrow—not a happy verdict on a decade of training!

Chemistry is a practical subject: we all reiterate this so often and it seems quite normal to us to require a student to spend long hours in the laboratory. In the past it was possible for a student to become skilled in manipulative and other practical techniques which he could subsequently use *directly* in either his research or his professional career. But now two difficulties clearly arise. First, training in manipulation and in the making of disciplined and intelligent measurements must be telescoped with the need to acquire yet more knowledge—in other words, a student cannot first learn his skills and then apply them to chemical experiments. Secondly, the skills and techniques which he *does* learn may no longer be so directly applicable to his postgraduate work either in research or professionally, and in any case are likely to be out of date before he has reached the mid-point of his professional chemical career. Quite often, a student emerges from a present day chemistry course with a rather inadequate grasp of experimental technique, with a rather random knowledge of practical chemistry, and with the view that it is all a bit useless after he has finished. In fact, this view is probably too pessimistic—he has probably learned quite a lot, and the value of what he has learnt will become apparent later—*if* he continues to be a practising chemist. So despite many shortcomings, the practical course will have had value for some. It is in any circumstances difficult to define how a person is to be 'trained' for research in chemistry, because research can mean so many things. Nor is it really clear how someone is to be adequately 'trained' for employment as a chemist; the Eaborn Report implied, in very general terms, that the present kind of training is not bad. But because employment as a chemist is not by any means as certain as it was for the new graduate in chemistry, it is surely no longer appropriate to think of a chemistry course exclusively in terms of a subsequent career as a chemist, research or otherwise.

If then some or all of these requirements I have listed are no longer valid, what new kind of chemistry curriculum should be developed? There are two provisos that must be made before attempting an answer to this question. The first is that, whatever changes are made, something like the present degree course in chemistry must remain, perhaps in some greatly improved form, but unchanged in its essentials. This is because the present system does provide, to the best of our knowledge, an adequate training for the enthusiastic chemist—the research worker-to-be, the practising chemist. The second proviso is that any new type of chemistry curriculum will unavoidably come up against the criticism that 'it is of lower standard'. This of course takes us immediately into problems of assessment, which do not really fall within the scope of my talk. All I wish to say on assessment is quite simple; it is that there is, to my knowledge, no valid objective way of comparing standards in Chemistry with those in (say) Economics or History and therefore there is no objective way of comparing standards in 'traditional' Chemistry with those in any kind of 'new' Chemistry curriculum which might be devised. What must be done to validate the standard of a new curriculum is to see that it is carefully thought out in terms of aims and objectives, that it is taught by interested and involved people, and (most importantly) that it is assessed in an effective and searching way with appropriate external moderation of some kind. Even when all this has been done the accusation of a lower standard will still be made. Experiences with new curricula at school level (e.g. Nuffield Chemistry) suggest that the pass rate in a new curriculum is often decidedly higher than that achieved in the corresponding conventional curriculum. This naturally causes many to say that the new curriculum is too easy. But it must be remembered that new curricula are usually taken up first by educational institutions with enthusiastic staff and which have students who are equally enthusiastic and well-motivated. So an increased pass rate on a new curriculum must not be taken as the only criterion of its standard.

I have referred to new chemistry curricula at schools rather deliberately, because their development points the way for the first change which we may need to make at the tertiary level. Formerly, school chemistry curricula were written down in terms of content; a new Nuffield-type chemistry course cannot be written down in this way, simply because it has been formulated in terms of aims and objectives, with content as a subsidiary consideration. It is partly because of this approach that new Nuffield-type courses have often been regarded with suspicion and dislike by teachers of more orthodox courses—the conventional teacher is anxious that his students should 'know about' this or that. Therefore any new kind of tertiary chemical course may, quite probably, not be definable in terms of content, and therefore will not provide the prospective graduate with an overall knowledge of chemistry. So this consequence of a non-comprehensive course has to be reckoned with—its content may be ill-defined.

Secondly, this new type of course may not be practical in the sense that a conventional course is practical. Practical chemistry is a joy for some, a necessity for others, and disliked by those who find manipulative and other practical skills difficult. For those who enjoy it, practical work must remain as an essential part of a chemistry course but, for those who do not enjoy the purely experimental part of chemistry, is it not possible to design some *simulated* experiments, in which the student must still make decisions, select data, interpret such things as spectra, correlate observations and comment on results—all without requiring purely experimental skills? Participation in such 'experiments' would enable the student at least to appreciate and evaluate the rôle of practical work in chemistry, and to view its results critically. For those who dislike practical work generally some more radical change might be appropriate, perhaps for them a new chemistry curriculum much more akin to that of an Arts subject would be suitable. This theme of 'Arts-type' chemistry course was developed very successfully in a notable talk by Prof. Norman Greenwood given at the British Association meeting in Cardiff in September, 1971.

Thirdly, the new type of course may not be so demanding in terms of what the student has done previously. Many tertiary chemistry courses have demanded 'A level qualifications in Mathematics and Physics as well as in Chemistry; the school-undergraduate-postgraduate decade of training for a research chemist has often required the study of Physics and/or Mathematics to be done over about half that period. So the training of the conventional chemist is not only lengthy and comprehensive but requires other subjects as well. I suspect that many who will wish to study chemistry in the future will either not have had the opportunity—or (more probably) not had the inclination—to study Mathematics and Physics at school, and certainly therefore will not wish to start these admittedly difficult subjects at the tertiary level. Is it therefore too much to ask that serious consideration be given to a course in chemistry appropriate to non-mathematical and 'non-physical' entrants? I can almost feel the horror of my audience at such a suggestion—what, no physical chemistry, no quantum mechanics, no thermodynamics? But surely most of us have at some time had to teach some sort of chemistry to biologists, or to medical students, or to others whose mathematical/physical qualifications are insignificant. Can we not teach the same sort of chemistry in its own right? It is true that much effort has been going into attempts to integrate the three traditional branches of chemistry; it is equally true that real success in these efforts is so far lacking at school level, and is certainly far from apparent at the tertiary level. It is perhaps significant that a UNESCO survey[1] of developments in chemistry at university level has shown that, while most countries are intent on the integration of chemistry, there are some countries where physical chemistry is being hived off in association with physics (to become physical science), or where chemistry is being sub-divided into branches, which can be quite separately studied according to the choice of the student.

By now, you may feel that our familiar existing chemistry course has been maimed and mangled beyond recognition. Is there anything worthwhile that is left? Certainly, there is a lot of *space* left in the curriculum—and that has been the deliberate reason for my butchery. We now have to use the space made available for appropriate components of our new chemistry course. What are these to be? In the opinion of many, these components could be summarized under one heading, namely *relevance* (I apologize for having to use this overworked word!). Chemistry must be relevant to all other concerns of mankind, whether social, economic, philosophical or whatever. I would agree with this view; but to achieve relevance I think we need to give priority to another component of our course—*communication* (again an overworked but unavoidable word). We all know that students in non-science disciplines must acquire skill in communication as readily as the chemist learns his formulae and equations—his own means of communication with his fellow-chemists—but whereas the Arts or Social Science graduate learns, necessarily, to communicate with others outside his discipline, the chemist becomes ever more deeply immersed in his own strange jungle characterized by a lush growth of increasingly complex terms and nomenclature. Until recently, a glance at a list of talks on the radio or features on television, or a list of extension lectures, revealed the conspicuous absence of pure science topics. I say 'until recently' because The Open University is, by necessity, breaking though this communication barrier between scientists and the rest of the world, and giving us much to think about in the process, because we *all* need to consider carefully how we can equip our new chemists to communicate. For example, at Liverpool we are constructing a new course, tentatively called 'Science Communication', in which a team of lecturers drawn from departments of science, education, extension studies and audio-visual aids are cooperating; the aim of the course is to enable students in the various pure sciences to communicate first of all with each other and then with the outside world. They will be given many diverse problems in communication, and it is hoped that sample 'audiences' of very varied kinds can be found for them to achieve practice in communication. Necessarily, this course at present is ancillary to traditional degree courses in the sciences; ultimately, I believe, it must become an integral part of new science courses. Already however it has shown the value of a cooperative effort, traditional science teachers working with educationists and others to synthesize a course. I think this kind of cooperation and integration is vital if communication is to be built into chemistry courses; we shall ourselves need to learn a great deal about it. There are several encouraging signs of such cooperation already; for example, in the vocational B.Ed. degree chemists have been prominent in seeking integration between the chemistry and education components.

Communication, then, is seen as an essential prerequisite of relating chemistry to humanity. It will need to be encouraged and fostered at all stages and in all areas of the new chemistry curriculum. It will probably imply quite different lectures and certainly will require different tutorials; it will need its own equivalent of practical work, and it most certainly will make heavy demands on both staff and students—as already emphasized, it must not be seen as a 'soft option'. It will need consultation with industry, and especially with people like university appointments officers or career advisers, who have been among the most outspoken critics of conventional chemistry courses, chiefly because (I think) they see the inadequacy of such courses for the careers which chemists must now seek out. It is they who can help us in specifying the ways in which chemists must now learn to communicate. Perhaps indeed relevance and communication will need some attention at the secondary as well as at the tertiary level. Many school pupils are anxious, or indeed eager, to appreciate the relevance of their science especially to the social and environmental problems which rightly disturb them. Attempts are now being made at G.C.E. 'A' level to introduce a syllabus in chemistry where applied chemistry is studied, not only as an important part of chemistry but also in relation to the problems it can create—or solve—through the medium of case-studies. Communication will be seen as a vital link in this relationship.

Chemistry and the other sciences are today regarded by the man in the street not only with respect (which still remains) but with increasing suspicion and indeed with fear. There must be a break out from our closed-shell science and an awareness of the problems of relevance and communication; what better way of achieving this than by educating our future chemists to achieve this breakthrough?

Reference

1. A. K. Holliday and R. Maskill (Eds.), *Survey of Chemistry Teaching at University Level,* UNESCO/IUPAC, Oxford 1972.

CHAPTER 6

A New Practical Course in Inorganic Chemistry

B. O. FIELD

The need for a fresh orientation in the teaching of practical chemistry has attracted a good deal of attention in recent years. In a typical honours degree course in chemistry, the amount of time allocated to the laboratory normally takes up at least 50 per cent of the total course time. It has been suggested[1,2] that new courses should be developed with a reduced amount of laboratory time, but there is general agreement that any tertiary chemistry course must give the student some laboratory experience. The nature of this experience will obviously be determined by the overall objectives of the course, but whatever the objectives, it seems clear that there is a need for a re-appraisal in the chemistry departments of the nature and content of laboratory work[3,4]. The objectives of a laboratory course, if they are expressed at all, usually consist of such statements as 'to illustrate the principles and applications developed in the lecture course', or 'to give the student experience of a range of practical tech niques'. These statements reflect the teacher-centred attitudes which have been typical until very recently; the student is considered as the raw material which is processed in a number of ways during his chemistry course and emerges at the end equipped for his role as a professional chemist. However, there are new requirements, new student attitudes, and new patterns in chemistry which must now determine the nature of chemistry courses. The 'Eaborn degree'[5,6] represents a radical break with tradition, an attempt to place the student, rather than the teacher, at the centre of the teaching/ learning situation. In a more modest way, we have tried to take account of these new requirements in the design of a new course in practical inorganic chemistry at Part 1 level.

COURSE OBJECTIVES

1. To give the student a perspective of modern inorganic chemistry on the basis of structure-reactivity relationships.

2.   To expose the student to a wide range of instrumental structural and analytical techniques.

3.   To stimulate the student into orientating his chemistry on a structural mechanistic basis. To ask the question 'why . . .?' and design an experiment to answer his question.

4.   To enable the student to discuss orally, and by a written report communicate, his experimental observations and his interpretation of them.

5.   To gain experience of working in a team, and of the individual and collective responsibilities that teamwork entails.

6.   To adopt a healthy critical attitude towards experimental data and the deductions based on them.

7.   The course must be adaptable for both the Nuffield and the non-Nuffield A-level entry.

STRUCTURE

It is possible to achieve these objectives in more than one way. We used as the integrating theme the main bond characteristics encountered in inorganic molecules as illustrated by the various properties of element-chlorine bonds. Four compounds, $NaCl$, CCl_4, $SiCl_4$, and $CrCl_3$ were chosen to illustrate a range of structure and properties. The student is asked to discover the physical and chemical manifestations of the bond type in these four compounds. In the first part of the course, the student carries out some experiments himself and uses data from other techniques (such as X-ray diffraction), which are too difficult to obtain for himself at this stage (*see* Appendix). At the end of this part of the course the student has to reach conclusions about the bond properties of the four reference compounds, and write a review co-ordinating the evidence from all the techniques listed in the appendix which supports his conclusions. In the second part of the course, the student explores in turn the chemical manifestations of each of the bond types he has deduced from the first part (*see* Appendix, p. 48). Each student does not carry out every experiment, but works as part of a group, at the end of the course, he must write an integrated account of the work carried out by the group, and its conclusions.

ORGANIZATION

The total timetable allocation for the course is 90 hours, made up of two 3 hour periods each week. The first part of the course, the investigation of the physical manifestations of bond type, is allotted a total of 30 hours, and the remainder of the time is spent on the second section. Most students, however put in additional time such as lunch breaks, sports periods etc. The students work in groups of four or five under the supervision of a staff member or a graduate demonstrator. At the beginning of a piece of work, the group meets under the chairmanship of the supervisor, to allocate the work in hand to particular students, and to set a deadline for its completion. Manipulative details for each experiment are given as handouts, together with a theoretical introduction if this is likely to be unfamiliar to the student. However, each student is expected to liaise closely with the group leader (demonstrator) on all matters pertaining to the design, manipulative details, and results of each experiment as well as on the theory and objectives of each assignment. At the end of each section of the course, the group holds seminars at which the individual members describe the work carried out and their conclusions. Each student writes up, in detail, the experiments that he personally carried out, and also an overall account of the work of the group.

The total mark assigned to this practical course is based on the written report (60%), contributions during seminars (20%), and practical ability (20%). The assessment in all cases is made by the group leader. Initially, the latter two subjective sections were independently marked by two assessors, but the similarity of the two sets of marks has led us to abandon this duplicate procedure.

RESULTS

All the course objectives enumerated above have been achieved to some extent. Students have developed a much greater sense of involvement during the course, as evidenced by the decrease in absenteeism and the amount of free time spent in the laboratory. The oral seminar contributions start off very hesitantly but rapidly improve as a result of ruthless criticism by student peers. The structure of the course places emphasis on team work, and this is probably the most important factor contributing to the effectiveness of the course. A student will try to avoid losing esteem within his own peer group, and this is a powerful motivator. We have found that criticism of a student's work or approach by his fellow students is much more effective than staff criticism, since students are much more critical of one another than the most demanding staff member.

Not all the changes resulting from the introduction of this course have been greeted with unanimous approval. Nearly twice as many staff/demonstrators are required than for a traditional course, and they must get involved in the course; sitting at the supervisors table throughout the laboratory period marking scripts, is no longer acceptable, or even possible, if the course is to succeed. As would be expected the analytical expertise is not as well developed as in the traditional course which contains much wet analytical work; but does this really matter now? One unexpected result was that some students spent a disproportionate amount of time on this course to the detriment of their other studies; however, this is a feature of project work in general.

CONCLUSIONS

This approach arose from scathing criticism of a previous traditional course containing single unrelated exercises and analytical work on the classical pattern. The students work much harder now, but enjoy the extra involvement that the new arrangement enforces and, to quote a phrase from the student report on the course it was received by them with 'unreserved unanimous approval'. It is recognized that this course will not train a student in a particular practical technique, but by adopting the practical-tutorial approach described above, we hope that he will achieve a grasp of the fundamentals of modern inorganic chemistry at an earlier stage in his academic life than with the older pattern of practical work.

References

1. A. K. Holliday, *Aims, Methods and Assessment in Advanced Science Education,* D. E. Billing and R. S. Furniss (Eds.), Heyden & Son, London 1973, p. 39 (this volume).
2. N. N. Greenwood, *Chemical Education at the Tertiary Level,* (Swansea symposium), The Chemical Society, London 1971, p. 15.
3. A. K. Holliday and W. J. Hughes, *Chem. Brit.* 7, 208 (1971).
4. T. J. Stone, *Chemical Education at the Tertiary Level,* (Swansea symposium 1971), The Chemical Society, London 1971, p. 35.
5. C. Eaborn, *Chem. Brit.* 6, 330 (1970).
6. C. Eaborn, *Aims, Methods and Assessment in Advanced Science Education,* D. E. Billing and B. S. Furniss (Eds.), Heyden & Son, London 1973, p. 65 (this volume).

APPENDIX

TO DISCOVER THE PHYSICAL MANIFESTATIONS OF BOND TYPE

The student examines data on NaCl; CCl_4; $SiCl_4$ and $CrCl_3$ (and, where possible, runs the experiment himself) from the following techniques:

1. X-ray diffraction data—electron density contour maps provided.
2. Melting point.
3. Electrical conductances in solid and liquid states.
4. Infrared spectra.
5. UV—visible spectra.
6. Mass spectra.
7. Magnetic properties.
8. Solution properties—pH of aqueous solutions molar conductances, etc.
9. Molecular weights—in the vapour phase from mass spectral data; in solution, by ebulliometry.
10. Models—polystyrene spheres used for ionic and modelling balloons for covalent structures.

TO DISCOVER THE CHEMICAL MANIFESTATIONS OF BOND TYPE

I.   Predominantly Ionic e.g. NaCl

   (*a*)   Preparation of a sodium polyhalide and its thermal decomposition. The polyhalide and its pyrolysis product is examined by infrared, uv and visible spectroscopy. The halogens present are identified by thin layer chromatography and estimated volumetrically and gravimetrically.

   (*b*)   The principles of Isotope Dilution Analysis are deduced by adding $^{86}Rb^+$ ions to a mixutre of Rb, Li and Na chlorides; and precipitating $^{86}Rb/Rb$ [B Ph_4].

   (*c*)   The relative sizes of the hydrated Group One metal ions are estimated by their R_f values determined by paper chromatography.

   (*d*)   The student is asked to try to change the oxidation state of e.g. Na.

   (*e*)   The student is asked to design experiments to determine if the Group I metal halides will form complexes with donor ligands.

II. *Predominantly Covalent, no acceptor properties e.g. CCl₄*

(*a*)   The chlorinating properties of CCl_4 at high temperatures and its use in the preparation of transition metal chlorides is illustrated by the student passing CCl_4 vapour in a stream of nitrogen over a fluidized bed of ZrO_2. The $ZrCl_4$ produced is quantitatively estimated and the student is asked to determine the experimental parameters (e.g. CCl_4/N_2 flow rate; temperature of fludized bed; oxide particle size etc.) necessary to optimize the yield of $ZrCl_4$; under high temperature/high flow rate conditions some $ZrCl_3$ is also produced.

(*b*)   The effects of strong oxidizing and reducing reagents on CCl_4 are investigated.

(*c*)   Attempts are made to form complexes of CCl_4 with donor ligands.

III. *Predominantly Covalent with acceptor properties e.g. SiCl₄.*

(*a*)   The greater reactivity of $SiCl_4$ compared to CCl_4 and the expansion of the coordination number from 4 to 6 in the second row of the Periodic Table is illustrated in the reactions of CCl_4 and $SiCl_4$ with acetylacetone. $[Si(acac)_3]$ Cl.HCl and $[Si(acac)_3]$ $[FeCl_4]$ are prepared and analysed.

(*b*)   Silicone polymers, cyclic and linear polysiloxanes are prepared from dimethyl-dichlorosilane. The student is asked to suggest a mechanism for the hydrolysis of dimethyldichlorosilane and to identify infrared bands due to Si-C and to Si-O bonds in his products.

IV. *Predominantly Covalent with acceptor properties and variable oxidation state of the metal e.g. CrCl₃; FeCl₃.*

(*a*)   The reduction of Cr(III) to Cr(II) is investigated and the Cr(II) compound is analysed quantitatively and its magnetic susceptibility and infrared spectra used to suggest a structure.

(*b*)   The uv and visible absorption spectra of complexes with a variety of different ligands bonded to Cr are determined in order to deduce the spectrochemical series.

(*c*)   The use of liquid ammonia in the preparation of some coordination complexes of Cr(III) illustrates some of the principles of non-aqueous solvent chemistry

The ionic conductance, infrared spectra and magnetic susceptibility together with quantitative analytical data are used to suggest structures for the products.

CHAPTER 7

Concurrent Courses in Education and Chemistry

I. F. ROBERTS

The Colleges of education have for many years been offering the concurrent study of chemistry and education as part of a professional course of training leading to the Certificate in Education. More recently, suitable candidates from over thirty such institutions have been able to continue the study of chemistry and education for a further year to obtain the Bachelor of Education degree. However, we shall be concerned here with a more recent development, the growth of concurrent courses in chemistry and education as an integral part of a university degree course.

THE COURSES

Such courses which are available at first degree and at graduate level are summarized in Table 7.1. Ten universities at present offer combined degree courses in which the study of education is a major component; of these, eight offer chemistry and educa-

Table 7.1. University Degree Courses which include the Concurrent Study of Education

---

1. *Educational Studies as a major component of the degree*
   1.1 Combined first degree courses
       ASTON, BATH, Brunel,[a] *CAMBRIDGE, CHELSEA,* LOUGHBOROUGH, *KEELE, STIRLING,* Surrey,[a] *ULSTER, YORK.*
   1.2 Combined higher degree courses
       SUSSEX
       All the above courses incorporate a professional training element.

2. *Concurrent Professional Training course alongside degree Course*
   2.1 First degree course
       KEELE
   2.2 Ph.D course
       KEELE, LEICESTER

---

[a] Course under discussion.

AMA—5

tion as one of the possible combinations. All courses include the opportunity to gain a professional teaching qualification as an integral part of the course, in addition to obtaining an honours degree. Normally the courses last four years; an exception is the course at the University of Stirling which is based on a 4-year honours degree, and requires 4½ years for honours and 3½ years for the general degree. It is noteworthy that nine of the ten universities offering concurrent courses are new universities, and that six out of the nine are technological universities with a sandwich course tradition. In addition, the University of Keele has from the outset run an option initial training course concurrently with first degree studies; and more recently, chemists working for their Ph.D at both Keele and Leicester can opt for an initial training course concurrently with such studies.

The structure and content of the courses vary widely, but in general, the chemistry and educational studies are distributed throughout the four years. At Keele, however, where we have a common Foundation Year Course, the education studies are largely confined to the remaining three 'principal' years (Table 7.2). Cambridge alone delays educational studies until the third year. All the courses provide teaching practice experience at the secondary level and a few, including Keele, offer experience in further education. The teaching practice varies in duration, concentration and incidence; normally it takes place during the third year of the course, but Keele (3 units of four weeks in the vacations) and York (two terms during the fourth year) are exceptions. Two universities, Aston and Surrey, make arrangements for the teaching experience to be conducted by a nearby College of Education. Typically, the teaching practice can be regarded as the equivalent of the industrial training component of the 'thick' sandwich course.

Table 7.2. University of Keele—Joint Honours Course in Mathematics and Science
          Education (B.A. with Certificate in Education)

	Year 1	Foundation Year			
TP 1	2	Education	Chemistry or Geology or Mathematics or Physics	Subsidiary	Subjects[a]
TP 2	3				
TP 3	4				

[a] Alternatively one subsidiary subject may be studied in each of the first and second Principal years.

Three year course in Mathematics and Science Education available from 1973 (B.Sc.).

TP = Teaching Practice

As one would expect, the relative weighting of the two subjects varies with the institution; at Keele, chemistry occupies 50 per cent of the course, and at York and Stirling 70 per cent. The Chemistry component is normally based on the regular courses in the chemistry department. At Keele, the course is identical to the chemistry course followed in combination with any other subject, and at York, it is essentially the same as that studied by those taking a single subject degree, but with a reduced subject content (especially in the later stages). The education component of all courses, irrespective of university, includes the following elements: psychology, sociology, philosophy, curriculum studies, history and administration, and educational technology. The approach, the time allotted to each topic, and the sequence are subject to wide variation between universities. Other subject areas offered include comparative education and statistics. The course at Keele emphasizes 'Mathematics and Science Education' (*see* Table 7.3).[1]

Table 7.3. University of Keele—The Principal Education Course

Principal Year 1	1. Mathematics and Science Education
	  (*a*) Curriculum Development
	  (*b*) Concept Development
	  (*c*) Teaching Maths, Science and Technology
	2. Introduction to Psychology and Sociology of Education
	3. The Educational System in England and Wales

Principal Year 2	1. Teaching One's Specialist Subject 2. Philosophy of Education 3. Further Psychological and Sociological Studies 4. Education and Industry 5. Educational Research Methods
Principal Year 3	1. Curriculum Studies 2. The Sociology of Science and the Sociology of Curriculum 3. The Nature and Development of Scientific Knowledge 4. Educational Research

The University of Sussex offers a postgraduate course combining a D.Phil. in chemistry with the Certificate in Education. The objectives of the course are twofold: firstly, to enable a student to take a research degree in chemistry and at the same time to prepare himself for a school-teaching career, by gaining a recognized teaching qualification; and secondly, to encourage the production of qualified teachers of chemistry who possess research experience. The joint programme is regarded as a single entity. Thus, a student who fails to qualify for the Certificate in Education will not normally be allowed to carry on working for the D.Phil. in chemistry.

Many readers will also be conversant with the existence of the research group in chemical education at the University of East Anglia. This group, which is based within the Department of Chemical Sciences offers a course of graduate study leading to an M.Sc. in Chemical Education, as well as an optional minor course in the subject at the undergraduate level. King's College London also offer an M.Ed. in Science Education which is at present confined to co-ordinated studies in chemistry and education. All these courses differ from the others referred to, in that they do not include an element which is specifically orientated towards a professional qualification in teaching.

EDUCATION AS A DEGREE SUBJECT

The total number of degree courses in which education is a major conponent is
a very small proportion of all combined degree courses currently advertised. One
reason for this may be that many academics see the study of education as predominantly a vocational training which has no place in a degree course. Even
assuming this to be so, it is difficult to understand why the same academics see
no inconsistency in accepting medicine as part of the university degree system.

A second problem associated with degree courses, which include education as a
major component, is the possible restriction of career opportunities for such
graduates. Graduates who undertake a postgraduate certificate in education course
normally do so because they have made up their minds to teach. It is clear that
combined degree courses in education and another subject need not necessarily
jeopardize a student's prospects of a career in his second subject. Thus at Keele, the
chemistry component is identical with that in any other subject combination, and
students who achieve the required standard in chemistry may, if they so desire, undertake research in chemistry (since the S.R.C. recognizes joint degrees as qualifying for
graduate awards). Such an approach certainly allows students to keep their options
open.

There is evidence,[2] from the University of York, to show that education students
are in no way prevented from specializing further in science after graduation. In any
case, the majority of courses delay the registration for the teaching certificate course
until the end of the second year. Furthermore, as was recently pointed out by Sir
Frederick Dainton, 'Scientists will have to accept that their degree can be used as an
entry into a number of areas which have nothing to do with science.'[3]

EDUCATION AND CHEMISTRY

The structure of joint degree studies necessitates close co-operation between the staff
of other departments concerned. At Keele and York, education lecturers are members
of the science Boards of Studies, and at York the joint courses are handled by a small
executive committee representative of the two departments concerned. The importance of such close liaison cannot be overemphasized, and its benefits also extend, for
example, into the area of in-service training through the Teachers' Centres. This close
liaison can allow parts of the chemistry course to be used as a basis for educational
studies. Thus, their practical chemistry exercises can be used by the students as a basis
for the design of a valid assessment scheme; or recent studies of the transition elements
in chemistry can be used as a background to the teaching of the d-block elements at
'A' level.

The study of a single science subject in the concurrent degree course is undoubtedly
of value to the student, but it is also important to bear in mind the need for teachers
to have a broad understanding of science rather than a narrow specialization. Important changes in our patterns of teaching are associated with the growth of comprehensive schools with an emphasis on 'mixed ability' teaching, and the development of
integrated schemes such as Nuffield Combined Science, the Schools Council Integrated
Science, and Nuffield 'A' level Physical Science. Furthermore, a chemist who is Head

of Science in a large comprehensive school where Nuffield Secondary Science is taught
will be faced with an integrated scheme in which chemistry, as a discipline in its own
right, is of very minor importance. In this context, concurrent courses are vulnerable
unless care is taken to allow students, who so desire, to study other aspects of science
at some point during the course. The proposed course at Chelsea, with its variable
course unit approach, provides a great deal of flexibility in this respect. Moreover, the
University of Stirling offers education in combination with integrated science.

ADVANTAGES OF COMBINED DEGREE COURSES

(i) The pursuit of education as a component of the degree course coupled with the
opportunity to prepare for the Certificate in Education provides depth and breadth of
study well beyond that which is possible within the conventional one-year postgraduate certificate in education course.

(ii) Combined honours courses in education and chemistry can meet a variety of
vocational needs: (*a*) hopefully, these courses will be as successful as those in
chemistry and economics in providing personnel for industry (and in particular, the
educational side of industry); (*b*) some of the best candidates could, on completion of
further specialist studies in chemistry, progress to university teaching or teaching
within further education. The need for professionally qualified teachers in further
education is gradually being recognized, and as has been shown elsewhere,[4] the
universities have a contribution to make in this important field of teacher training, (*c*)
at a recent meeting of the National Foundation for Educational Research, Professor
William Taylor spoke as follows: 'We cannot rely on the existing pool of experienced
teachers as a source of future educational researchers . . . A larger proportion of young
graduates with sound knowledge and understanding of one or more of the social
sciences, together with appropriate research skills should be recruited'. The current
NFER policy is based on all its recruits having two to five years classroom experience
as a prerequisite to appointment. Combined degree courses in education and a science,
particularly where they include an introduction to research methods, could well help
to relieve the staffing difficulties of our research institutions.

(iii) Today many undergraduates show their concern for the society in which they
live by wishing to relate their science with some aspect of social study. Combined
degree courses in education and science can meet this need and should help to channel
some of our reluctant sixth-form scientists back into science, as they offer an approach
not previously available.

THE FUTURE

Although we have, in educational studies an interdisciplinary approach which can
provide both breadth and depth, education as a component of combined degree
courses is still a relatively new field of study. One component of such studies is
chemical education, which is in itself a rapidly developing area. Aims and objectives
have to be so defined as to be meaningful to other people. Curriculum reform, particularly when based on the use of curriculum models, provides a basis on which to relate

theory and practice. Assessment and evaluation procedures are gradually being developed so that they stand up to statistical scrutiny, and more recently attempts are being made to place the conceptual framework of chemistry on a sound basis. Inevitably such developments further stimulate the growth of research in the field of chemical education.

At present, chemistry is one of twenty-four different subjects which can be combined with education at first degree level, and it is likely that the range of subjects will increase. The emphasis on scientific subjects is strong, and chemical education will undoubtedly continue to be an important growth point in the future.

The phenomenal growth of combined degree courses has been one of the major changes in the pattern of university courses during the last few years, and today they rank alongside single-honours courses as viable alternatives. Combined degree courses, in education and mathematics or a science, are however, still very much in their infancy as many courses have yet to produce their first graduates. Yet impressions to date are very favourable and indicate that, in general, educational studies are based predominantly on an approach which is not only educationally stimulating and rigorous in method, but also flexible in content.

References

1. I. F. Roberts, D. A. Tawney and F. R. Watson, *School Sci. Rev.* **53**, 199 (1971).
2. I. Smith, C. F. Stoneman and G. R. Walker, *School Sci. Rev.* **53**, 208 (1971); G. R. Walker, personal communication.
3. F. Dainton, *Chem. Brit.* **7**, (11) (1971).
4. I. F. Roberts and L. M. Cantor, *Teacher Training and Further Education* (Occasional Publication), Department of Education, University of Loughborough 1971.

CHAPTER 8

A 'Science Greats' Course at Manchester

J. RONAYNE

It is relatively well known that the majority of our qualified scientists and engineers in industry and in Government service in Britain are not engaged in activities which could be classed as Research and Development (R & D). In industry they are a part of what Galbraith[1] has called the technostructure, the body of educated manpower engaged in the decision-making process in corporate management. The technostructure is organized intelligence; under this heading come the people who contribute items of specialized knowledge and experience to the decision-making process—scientists, engineers, designers, technical managers, production managers, marketing specialists, operations researchers and so on. In general the specialized knowledge and experience which are contributed by such people derives little from their formal education and training at the tertiary level.

Now the management culture is said to embody certain features which are at variance with the cultural ideology of pure science. Financial soundness, conformity with established policies and procedures, tangible private rewards within the hierarchical structure, loyalty to the organizations and dedication to the profit motive are all said to be management characteristics. Diametrically opposed to this, the ethos of pure science encourages freedom of choice in work and methods, freedom of communication, freedom from financial accountability and primary loyalty to the advancement of certified knowledge.

Some American sociologists have asserted[2] that conflict of values occurs when scientists, with the academically oriented education and training are recruited into industry, but the work of Cotgrove[3] and Ellis[4] on scientists employed in British industry shows that this assertion cannot be upheld without some modification. Nevertheless, it does indicate that there was a real need for the attempts in the sixties to examine critically the structure and aims of our system of education in science to see if the needs of the individual and the needs of potential employing organizations could be more effectively matched.

The single honours degree concentrating on the study in depth of one subject with, perhaps, one or two subsidiary but related subjects thrown in has traditionally been the accepted pattern of higher education in British universities. Any student, the argument runs, who can master a scientific subject in depth, with the resultant training of the mind is well prepared for the real life situation, a situation where he may not actually need any of the knowledge he has acquired, but where the well-trained mind, disciplined by the rigorous study in depth of a scientific subject will enable him to pick up what he needs as he goes along. This argument has merit, it is true, but the fact is that this type of education is an excellent one for the production of academically inclined research scientists, those who actually use the storehouse of knowledge and skill that they have acquired to the best advantage. Whether or not it is the best type of education for the majority of our scientists who are destined to become a part of the industrial and Governmental technostructure is a moot point. Current disenchantment in some quarters with this type of narrow specialism is summed up in the following quotation:

> 'What is missing from the education of the present generation of scientists? First, they lack general education. They go out of their laboratories as learned ignoramuses knowing all about n.m.r., or the physiological function of A.T.P. but without any grasp of history, of philosophy, of political thought or of economics . . . We instil in our technologists the highest professional standards, so that they are rightly suspicious of the claims of anyone but an expert in their own field—and then we entrust them with tasks that demand expert judgement over many fields. We need science generalists not just to run big business or go into politics, but to do science itself . . . Our specialized courses of study—pure physics, pure chemistry, pure biochemistry, even pure medicine and pure engineering—are absurd and nonsensical as a training for active life.'[5]

Of course, this is an extreme view; there will always be a need for people who have the complete mastery of a subject to the limits of its accumulated knowledge and there will always be people who will feel dissatisfied or cheated unless they have been taken to the frontiers in their chosen subject. But the point is that this type of education need not, and should not, be all pervasive.

Recognizing the fact that specialist study alone at tertiary level was educationally inadequate and reinforced in their views by the observations of the man-power planners in the sixties that there was a need for generalists from the science side, a number of universities made provision in their curricula for broadening their existing courses and instituted entirely new courses designed to produce scientific non-specialists.

The foundation year at Keele is a radical and imaginative innovation not specifically aimed at the production of non-specialists but serves the educational function of allowing specialists from the sixth form to come into contact with ideas different from those of their specialism. Since the early sixties many courses have emerged which are designed with the non-specialist in mind and seem to achieve in their own way the objective of producing a well educated generalist with a knowledge of science and its social relations. Examples are the physical and human sciences course at Surrey, technological economics at Stirling, human sciences at Oxford and our own course, Liberal Studies in Science.

THE MANCHESTER APPROACH

The Faculty of Science at Manchester saw the problem in the following way:

> 'Of course we must go on producing professional scientists, engineers, economists, doctors and so on; but as society gets more technology based and technology more science based . . . there is an increasing need to provide the interpreters such as teachers, journalists, civil servants, industrial managers. But need these people be virtually the monopoly of the humanities, as has been usual in the past? Should not a proportion of them be brought up on the science side?'[6]

In principle such a proposition ought to command overwhelming assent but how does one go about devising a course for such a radical prescription? One can achieve breadth by grafting on to the existing structure of a specialist degree a course in an entirely unrelated discipline; or one might achieve it by a system of joint honours courses, constructed by juxtaposing halves of two existing single-subject Honours courses.

In Manchester the decision was made to create a new course within a new Department incorporating the educational ideas of breadth and depth to achieve a balance of skills in the graduate which would enable him to adapt the more readily to his role in society. Such a graduate should know what science is and what it can do and what effects it has on ordinary thinking. He should have a well developed sense of the aesthetic when observing the beautiful simplicity of the laws of nature or the more complex beauties of the jet engine or the living cell. He should be able to discuss problems of technological choice, for example, and be able to reason using scientific method. A liberal education can be described as an enlargement of the mind; in Whitehead's words, an education for thought and aesthetic appreciation; and the Manchester prescription was for the development of a *liberal education in science.*

It was clear, however, that some problems of integration might arise. The physical sciences as they are taught can be quite illiberal because the subject matter as presented to the student by its very nature allows for little dissent or constructive criticism. It is this unyielding certainty of the physical sciences which can give rise to problems of integration when the area with which it is to be integrated combines the historical, philosophical, sociological and economic study of science, an area of study in which the student can, at a much earlier stage, contribute in a constructive way to the discussion of open-ended issues, matching his polemical and interpretive skills against that of his teacher. The public image of the scientist, the objective seeker after the truth which is arrived at by certain procedures of empirical observation and hypothetico deductive logic, is the one which is shown to the student and which can be far from the truth. There is a qualitative difference between science as it is taught and science as it is produced. As F. R. Jevons has put it:

> 'In the process of converting research material into teaching material, a qualitative change tends to occur in the nature of intellectual processes. Discovery tends to turn into exposition, the spirit of enquiry into one of dogmatism, reasoning from evidence into remembering the stages of a proof.'[7]

But problems of integration are not unique to the sciences and the Faculty believed that the Politics, Philosophy and Economics course at Oxford could serve as an examplar. This is, perhaps, one of the earliest multidisciplinary courses, an integrated course with breadth and depth and stretching the students to the limit. Coherence and integration are achieved and require a lot of insight on the part of the student; the interconnections are there but they have to be sought. A course such as this was what the Faculty had in mind, producing graduates with attributes which are customarily associated with graduates in arts—facility of expression, flexibility of mind and literary ability. But they would have something else—numeracy.

The idea of numeracy complementing literacy was introduced in the Crowther report in 1959 and has now been enshrined in common educational terminology Numeracy is the ability to reason quantitatively, and acquaintance with the methods of science. Literacy includes, not only literary ability but also the development of moral, aesthetic and social judgement; the cultivation of extensive reading habits and the ability to select material from diverse sources to support arguments, might also be added.

THE MANCHESTER COURSE

Table 8.1 gives some idea of the course set up and I will talk firstly about the Liberal Studies in Science core. Science is more than a mere body of knowledge. From its origins in the 16th and 17th centuries, modern science has emerged as the most significant of human endeavours; it has profoundly affected the theory of knowledge and

Table 8.1

FIRST YEAR		
Physical Science	*Liberal Studies in Science*	*Subsidiary subject*
Physics of atoms and nuclei. Engineering thermodynamics, structures and metal processing	Technology in the economic development of Britain since 1700. Origins of modern science: internal and external factors	Chemistry for those who have *not* taken this subject to 'A' level; choice of physiology, psychology or geography for others
SECOND YEAR		
Physical Science	*Liberal Studies in Science*	
Wave phenomena, solid state physics and elementary particles. Chemistry Computer programming and logical design	Introduction to positive economics (includes dissertation). Social consequences of technology	
THIRD YEAR		
Physical Science	*Liberal Studies in Science*	*Thesis*
Energy processes and statistical thermodynamics. Chemistry	Case histories of technological projects. Science, technology and politics. Scientists and society	Each third year Honours student does an undergraduate thesis

has been responsible for the change in man's vision of himself and his universe and is, of course, the most potent source of change in our physical environment and our social and economic status.

The historical approach in the first year emphasizes the aspects of the scientific revolution which are of permanent relevance to science—the nature of the scientific method and of scientific knowledge, the organization of science and factors influencing the growth of science. There is, in addition, a course on the Economic History of Britain, given by a member of staff of the History Department which illustrates the role of science and technology in economic development.

In the second year the emphasis is on recent history and on economic factors in large projects where technological and social factors have to be taken into account. Technical innovation is studied in detail as well as factors in the transfer of technology, the importance of spin-off and the relationship between science, technology and wealth. The course on positive economics, given by the Department of Economics, includes some discussion on the various methods of project evaluation used in the course of investment decision making and cost-benefit analysis.

In the third year the sociological and political implications of science are considered together with some philosophical issues arising out of the debate on the way in which scientific knowledge accumulates. The scientific community now constitutes a major social group within society with its own norms and values, needs and responsibilities. It is intimately connected with Government, shaping national and international policies as they affect science; a major study of these political interactions is carried out in the third year with the co-operation of the Department of Government, which kindly lends us a lecturer specializing in this area. Lectures on some case-study material of technological innovation in industry, based on products which won the Queen's Award to Industry, examine the different management and personnel factors which influenced the innovations, the creative elements involved and the evaluation of project alternatives. These then, are the aspects of science which the students study in the 'liberal' core of the course; science is observed in its historical philosophical, sociological and political setting. Science is the focus of interest but without a knowledge of the systematics of science such a study could only be superficial

But the question may be asked whether such a study can really achieve intellectual rigor; it is our belief that it can and we take as our guideline another Oxford course in the Humanities, the Honour School in *Literae Humaniores,* known as *Greats.* This is a study of the ancient civilizations, its central core is linguistic and to this are added other aspects including the historical, philosophical and literary.

In our course, which is known colloquially as 'Science Greats', physical science is the central core. A fairly rigorous academic study of physics and chemistry together with engineering and computer science provides the framework within which science can be studied from the points of view already enumerated. The courses in the sciences are provided by the Departments of Physics, Chemistry, Engineering and Computer Science within the University.

The fact that the students are required to study the content of pure and applied science to a relatively high level ensures that their examination of the social relations of science is carried out in a more than superficial way. Philosophy, sociology, economics and history are all disciplines in their own right of course, but for our purposes they are mobilized to illuminate science in its social context. The social

relations of science as an area of knowledge is now developing as a specialized subject
to such an extent that we have been able to establish a postgraduate course in it for
graduates in science and technology and maintain a vigorous research programme in
the area.

A CURRENT APPRAISAL

In this paper I have tried to explain the underlying philosophy of the Department of
Liberal Studies in Science, a Department which was specially created to devise a
non-specialized science-based course to produce graduates who would, by virtue of
their training, be able to compete with advantage with graduates in the humanities and
with specialists in science and technology for jobs in which a specialized knowledge of
a single discipline is not an essential requirement. I believe that we can now claim
success in the venture; our student intake has increased from 13 in 1966 to 32 in 1971
and the total complement of the Department, including postgraduates and research
fellows stands in excess of 100. The graduates, who have been described by the Secretary of the Careers and Appointments Service at Manchester as 'some of the most
marketable students in the University' have had little difficulty in getting suitable jobs
in industry, commerce, teaching and academic research.

Our entry requirements include mathematics and physics at A-level and a third
A-level which can be in either a science or arts subject; candidates who do not have
chemistry at A-level are required to take chemistry as a subsidiary subject in the first
year. We can see little need for any alteration in our entry requirements at the present
time but there is the possibility that we will be able to introduce a set of parallel
courses based on the life sciences. When this scheme is instituted we will, of course
have to re-examine the range of acceptable subjects at Advanced level.

NATIONAL TRENDS

There has been a good deal of comment on the desirability of despecialization and the
reform of curricula at secondary and tertiary level but the trend towards the development of more broad-based courses in the British Universities is still far short of being
overwhelming. Suggestions for despecialization range from compulsory 'liberal' education for all in a two-year first degree[8] to the introduction of flexibility into existing
Honours courses.

But before generalist courses can become a completely acceptable alternative to the
traditional specialist degree course, the doubts which still linger as to their intellectual
and educational respectability must be allayed. At present there is some confusion as
to what is implied by the terms 'generalist' or 'broad-based' and this leads to the fear
that in some way 'standards' are being lowered. Standards as they are applied to the
structure of higher education in science, are invented with the specialist degree in
mind. Who can deny, however, that high intellectual standards can be achieved in ways
other than the study in depth of a single subject? We believe that it is as educationally
sound to study one thing in many ways—the ancient civilizations, science, political
institutions—as it is to study many things in one way. Depth and breadth are not

mutually exclusive and in Manchester we believe that a course in science and its cultural institutions has been constructed embodying them both.

References

1. J. K. Galbraith, *The New Industrial State,* Hamish Hamilton, London 1967.
2. W. Kornhauser, *Scientists in Industry,* University of California Press 1962, and references therein.
3. S. Cotgrove and S. Box, *Science, Industry and Society,* Allen & Unwin, London 1970.
4. N. Ellis, *Technol. & Soc.* **4**, 33 (1969).
5. J. M. Ziman, *Impact Sci. Soc.* **21**, 115 (1971).
6. Manchester University, *Faculty of Science Minutes,* 26 January 1965.
7. F. R. Jevons, *Advan. Sci.* **27**, 237 (1971).
8. A. B. Pippard, A. D. I. Nicol, A. B. Parkes and W. A. Deer, *Nature* **228**, 813 (1970).

CHAPTER 9

The First Year of the 'Degree by Thesis' Course at the University of Sussex

C. EABORN

In the Degree by Thesis course at Sussex,[1] a student after his first two terms at the University takes up a research project, which from then on constitutes his primary commitment. His degree class is based on the quality of his performance in this project and in essays and literature surveys on topics relevant to it. He is tested on the material of each term's lecture topics, but he has only to reveal a basic knowledge and understanding of this material for 70 per cent of the courses taken by conventional degree students; beyond that point his performance in these tests does not count towards his degree class. The first students started on this new type of course in April 1971, and have now completed exactly three terms on it; it is much too early to attempt a definitive appraisal of the overall degree of success of this new approach to undergraduate learning of chemistry, but some comments can be made as a result of the first year's experience.

Certain difficulties foreseen by critics did not materialize. In particular, the undergraduates did not, as some sceptics feared, prove to be incompetent and even dangerous in the research laboratory. On the contrary, because they accepted their limitations and approached matters with care and caution, they were less dangerous than some new, over-confident graduate students Most settled very quickly into the research laboratories in which they were located, and within a term were virtually indistinguishable in general laboratory behaviour from the graduates around them, an important contribution to this situation was made by selected postgraduate or post-doctoral workers, each of whom acted as a laboratory adviser to an undergraduate. On the whole, progress with projects has been at least as good as could have been expected, and it seems very likely that publishable work will be produced by several of them; although this was not, of course, a deliberate objective.

The location of the undergraduate with research groups in the research laboratories proved to be of great importance in giving them confidence and a feeling of belonging. Unfortunately, because of limitations of space, four students had to be assigned to an undergraduate laboratory for the first term in the course and it is probably not a coincidence that all three of those who left the new course after one term (*see* below) were in this group.

Some expected difficulties *did* materialize. In particular a lot of extra work was involved for a good proportion of the members of faculty; some of this was probably of a once-for-all nature, necessary to get such a novel scheme operating; but the fact that each student has to be dealt with individually, in almost all aspects of his work, will necessarily involve additional faculty time.

A strain was placed on the students by being the first participants in such a new type of course, because in moments of doubt they could not get reassurance from the knowledge that others before them had been successful in the new route to a degree and this probably contributed to the departure from the course of 4 of the original group of 13. After the first term, one left not because of any dissatisfaction with the course or his progress, but because he had changed his mind and wished to study biochemistry, for which the thesis route was not available, while two others switched back into the conventional chemistry course because they felt a need for the externally-imposed discipline of that mode of study. The fourth, who was making good progress with his project, switched back at the end of his second term because he found that he preferred to learn as much as possible of the material of the lecture courses and to get credit for so doing. We can expect such transfers always to occur, since not everyone will be suited to the new route. Perhaps it is too easy, however, to drop out; in what is possibly a temporary period of trouble with his project or doubt about his abilities, a student can switch to the seeming safety of the conventional route; whereas if switching were not so easy, or carried some penalty, he might well persevere and overcome his difficulties.

Among those still on the course there is a wide range of work patterns, which reflect student attitudes, and also, in some cases, differing advice from supervisor-tutors. Of two students I supervise personally, one attends all the lectures, seminars and problem classes, and does all the set work and recommended reading, while the other attends no lectures or set classes, and does the minimum reading of recommended texts required to reach a basic qualifying standard in the tests which are held at the beginning of each term. Both, so far, have passed all the tests. Indeed, a survey of the work habits of all the students indicates that there is no significant correlation between a student's attendance at lectures, etc., and success in the course tests.* The surveys also indicate that the students on the new course are spending distinctly more time each week of term on their work than does the average conventional student. They also study more in the vacations, even though their terms are longer than those of the conventional student. To me, making a subjective assessment, they seem to have become distinctly more mature and self-reliant than the ordinary student.

There has been some beneficial 'spin-off' for the conventional courses. Firstly as was foreseen as a possibility,[1] the atmosphere of change brought about by discussion of the new course and the disadvantages of conventional courses here stimulated the chemistry faculty at Sussex to re-think completely the structure of the conventional course, which will take on a very different appearance from October 1973. Again, the

* A graduate, Mr. Haydn Mathias, is carrying out a systematic study of the behaviour and performance of students on the course and making an evaluation of its success and limitations. I am grateful to him for some of the information presented in this chapter.

need to define (for the Degree by Thesis students) what we mean by a 'basic knowledge and understanding' of the various aspects of chemistry, and to decide how to test it, has raised some fundamental questions. Since it is a necessary feature of the new course that the students must be free, if they choose, to learn by their own reading rather than from lectures, it has been necessary to give them more detailed accounts of course contents and/or reading guides than have previously been issued; and it was recently very rightly decided that such information must, in future, be made available to conventional students.

In summary, the first year's experience has shown that the new approach is undoubtedly viable. Two or three years more will be needed to assess just how successful it can be but I am satisfied with the way it is going.

Reference

1. C. Eaborn, *Chem. Brit.* **6**, 330 (1970).

III. EDUCATIONAL TECHNIQUES

CHAPTER 10

Instructional Methods in Tertiary Science Education

L. R. B. ELTON

Instructional methods in tertiary education have changed and are changing largely as a result of the advent of self instruction. We are gradually but perceptibly getting away from the idea that all there is to university teaching is for the lecturer to stand in front of the audience and give forth, leaving it to the students to pick up what they may. But the question arises: 'should these new methods replace the teacher or just support him, or do a bit of both?' I would say that up to now the teacher has mainly used these new methods to support himself; it certainly has not led to any redundancy among teachers and it is exceedingly doubtful whether this would happen, because the production of instructional material of this type is, as we already know, a very time consuming process, and once the material has been prepared it is still necessary to manage the teaching and learning situation. In fact, there is one point of view that the teacher should more and more become an educational manager, a manager of resources, a manager of methods and materials which he will direct and produce as appropriate and in that way become very much more effective.

The classical teaching methods used in tertiary education can be divided into three groups, the lecture, the laboratory and small-group teaching, and while the lecture and the laboratory might be classified as one method each, small-group teaching is at least six methods under one heading and one of the most difficult areas in which to be at all precise. The developments in teaching methods in tertiary education can be conveniently discussed under these three headings, in each case considering new methods which have been used to support the teacher and those that have been used to replace him.

THE LECTURE

The provision of printed lecture notes[1] for some of the first year science courses at the University of Surrey has been in operation for eight years. These are printed on one side of the paper only so that the student can make notes on the other side on any additional material or clarification of the notes. The notes were initially printed on the right hand side, but this meant that the majority of students obscured the printed material when making notes, so we subsequently printed them on the left hand side.

One of the objections that has been raised against the use of printed lecture notes is that they tend to ossify the course, since there is an in-built resistance to change. On the contrary, however, all the printed lecture notes we have provided have undergone substantial modification since they were first introduced. One of the major contributing factors has been the discussions with fellow lecturers many of whom also provided lecture notes; this has also led to the integration of different parts of the course.

Having provided printed lecture notes, one hopes that this will in some way produce more efficient learning, but this is not at all obviously so. In the superficial sense it is more efficient because each student will have a correct set of lecture notes and does not have to devote all his attention during the lecture to taking everything down. But what is not obvious, and this is one of the strongest arguments against printed lecture notes, is that the student will learn more efficiently in this way; there is an argument that students will actually learn by taking notes but what evidence there is does suggest that the provision of printed lecture notes does help to improve the learning process.[2]

Audio recording has been used to supplement or replace lectures.[3] In one investigation the lecture was recorded directly on to cassettes which were made available in the library within two or three hours of the lecture, together with duplicated material which extended the printed lecture notes. Students used this quite extensively for revision purposes and for clarifying points in the lecture they had not fully understood. There is a possibility that the provision of this additional material will result in a decrease in lecture attendance; in fact this did not happen, but there is no reason, in principle, why we should be too concerned even if it did happen. If it is accepted that the purpose of the lecture is to provide an efficient method of learning for the student, and not just to provide satisfaction for the lecturer, then there is no reason why the student should continue to attend lectures if a more efficient method is available to him. But in order to replace the lecture it is necessary to go beyond audio recording; visual material must also be provided. Using the principle of doing things as cheaply as is consistent with the desired level of efficiency, we decided to use tape/slide presentations rather than video-recording. We provided a specially made booth in which the slide appeared automatically on a screen in front of the student at a predetermined time in the tape recording.

Our experiments in replacing the lecture by a tape/slide presentation brought to light some of the problems inherent in such drastic alterations of the traditional teaching methods. We replaced three lectures in a lecture course by tape/slide presentations, and although the students did equally well in the examinations following the course, they did not like the new method; they objected to it, they found it inhuman and so did the lecturer. Anyone who tries to develop these sophisticated instructional methods must always bear in mind that the customer resistance comes not just from the teachers but often from the student, and once this kind of resistance has been set up it is exeedingly difficult to overcome. There is a very real temptation to continue to use new methods if a large investment of time and money has been devoted to them, even when the new methods have been shown to be unpopular with students; this in itself is a strong argument for using the cheapest method.

The only activity in which all, or nearly all, students participate at the same time is the lecture; students will attend as a matter of course and it is almost impossible to prevent them from attending. One reason for this preference for the lecture is that it is a group activity which reassures the student, but probably more important is that the lecture is the only way in which the syllabus is defined for the student; he may not learn anything in the lecture but he discovers what he has to learn. When the lecturer is also the examiner, attending lectures is probably the only way for the student to find out what he is going to be examined on.

Our experiments with the modification and replacement of lectures have convinced us that most staff and students like lectures, although the reasons for this are sociological and psychological rather than educational. For this reason, it seems that the most successful developments will be those which embody new methods as adjuncts to the lecture, rather than as complete replacements.*

THE LABORATORY

A typical laboratory course consists of a cycle of experiments through which the student works during the course of the year; this often means that he must carry out an experiment before he is familiar with the appropriate theoretical background. One convenient way in which this difficulty can be overcome is to provide a programmed text so that the student can quickly learn the theory; we have also experimented with the use of tape/slide presentation to accomplish the same objective. These methods obviously support the teacher in the laboratory, but recently we have devised a series of self-service experiments which effectively replace the teacher. They are quite short, typically 20-30 minutes, and they have very specific, generally single objectives, such as to learn one principle, or to gain expertise in one technique.[4] This is in sharp contrast to the traditional laboratory experiment which is usually much longer and is meant to achieve a number of objectives simultaneously, but it is rarely clear to students, and sometimes to staff, which objectives are meant to be achieved by each piece of practical work.

In general the single-concept experiments were designed to achieve an understanding of a principle, rather than to achieve expertise in particular practical techniques. Four different methods have been used to present the single-concept experiments: conventional script with bench apparatus; programmed script with bench apparatus; audio tape recording with duplicated material and bench apparatus; simulated experiments using film-loops or tape/slide presentations.[5] In the simulated experiments the student does not actually use any apparatus, but uses data or information which is provided. In this connection we have designed a teaching booth which incorporates back projection on to tracing paper so that the student can record the progress of moving bodies.[6]

The response to these innovations in laboratory teaching methods has been encouraging; students liked them because the objectives were clearly stated, time was used more efficiently and there was more time for them to think. From the assessment

* See Note added in proof (p. 74).

of the staff involved, it seems that there is a greater acquistion of skill, knowledge and understanding from these experiments than from the conventional experiments.

SMALL GROUP TEACHING

An inquiry[7] into small group teaching methods in the University of London showed that most of the five hundred teachers questioned used small group sessions to discuss and clarify students' difficulties arising from lectures or other teaching situations. One method we have been using which allows individual discussion of problems, and lets each student progress at his own pace, is the Keller Plan.[8,9] The basis of the method, which is similar to the Dalton Plan used in England in the 1920s, is that the content of the course is broken down into small units or assignments, each of which represents about one week's work. The student works through a unit by himself and when he considers he has mastered the material in the unit he is given a test which he must pass in order to proceed to the next unit. Typically the assignments last about a week, longer in some cases, shorter in others, and thus the method allows each student to progress at his own pace. If the student fails the test at the end of a unit he is directed to further study before he takes a second test on the same unit. The Keller Plan has several advantages over the traditional instructional methods; firstly, the teacher can keep a close check on the progress of each student because every week he has to check a test which the student has done on a unit of work; this personal contact is likely to be more successful than the traditional tutorial since the student has thought about the subject material in advance. In this way individual difficulties are well documented, and an early warning system is provided for students with particular problems. Secondly, students retain a much greater proportion of the material using the Keller Plan; advantage could perhaps be taken of this to reduce the syllabus content, since we normally pass students in an examination who have a good knowledge of about 40 per cent of the syllabus.

A variety of staff-student contact situations are possible with the Keller Plan. The regular test sessions are the only time when the student normally attends, but additional periods are made available for re-testing or for further explanation of material which is proving difficult. In addition, about once every three weeks, we include a lecture which is designed to be inspirational. It does not link with a particular part of the course, since the students will be at different stages, but it is relevant to the course as a whole. The purpose of the lecture is to provide additional interest and not to convey subject matter, and therefore, it is not compulsory and only about half of the class attend. One of the problems with the Keller Plan is that one tends to talk only to those students who are having difficulties, since if the student works through the test and gets it all right, he is given his next assignment and there is no need for further discussion. In order to provide additional stimulus for the better student, it would probably be necessary to introduce a regular seminar, but as yet we have not introduced this into our course.

In some instances small group teaching can actually be replaced by a tape/slide presentation, and we have found this particularly effective in a non-standard teaching situation, namely in the library. All our new students are introduced to the library, and the librarian used to say the same things over and over again to different groups of students; now this is available as a tape/slide sequence and this enables the student to hear it again later if he has forgotten how to use the library.

ASSESSMENT

In the foregoing sections I have described the ways in which we have modified the traditional teaching situations. We have also done some work on the way in which assessment can be used to improve learning; this can be considered under two headings, pre-knowledge surveys, and self-tests.

The testing of students before they start on a particular teaching-learning experience is particularly important, but it is something that is hardly ever carried out. When they first come to university, students have been prepared in a variety of ways and have covered a range of subject matter; a pre-knowledge survey will show up any deficiencies which can then be eliminated by remedial study. This kind of situation is not limited to the first year of a course; at the beginning of subsequent years the assumption is frequently made that the student is familiar with all the previous year's work, an assumption which is often not justified. We have developed over the last few years a type of test which we call an item association test,[10] in which the students are asked to link an item in one list with one or two items in a second list as being particularly relevant. This very quickly shows up gaps of knowledge over the group as a whole. We used this test on a group of students on a course of mathematics for scientists, and we found that their appreciation of certain concepts was very imprecise and that they were quite unfamiliar with certain notations and words; this was particularly important since these were words and notations used regularly by lecturers in the courses they were attending, and this must have left the majority of students totally confused. This kind of approach also lends itself to remedial work, and we are developing a different kind of test to diagnose individual student difficulties.

One of the problems associated with the lecture method is that the lecturer has little information on the progress of the students or on the effectiveness of his lectures, and the students are uncertain of the amount and accuracy of their learning In order to provide ourselves with some feedback and the students with an indication of their progress, we devised a book of self-tests to accompany the course of lectures.* The students were provided with the answers to the tests to enable them to find out how they were getting on, and we were able to check the progress of the group as a whole, but not of the individual, by a show of hands in the lecture room; this also enabled the students to see how they were progressing relative to the other members of the class. The results of the tests are also handed in anonymously in written form so that the lecturer has a record of the progress of the group and can therefore assess which parts of the course are proving difficult for the students. The extent to which the tests have resulted in improved learning has not been easy to establish, but the vast majority of the students on the course used them at some time.

CONCLUSION

The introduction of many of the innovations I have discussed will mean that the lecturer will, in future, spend less of his time lecturing; there will still be much for him to do, although a good deal of it may not be as satisfying as actually standing in front of a student audience and talking to them. The role of the teacher will become more

* This has now been incorporated in a text book.[11]

and more that of a manager of the teaching and learning situation; if as a result, the students benefit then this new role must be accepted. University teachers have in the past tended too much to consider tertiary education as a teacher-centred rather than a student-centred activity; one of the most difficult tasks that must now be faced is to persuade one's colleagues of the value of the innovations and discoveries in educational technology over the past few years, some of which I have described.

Acknowledgements

My thanks are due to D. J. Boud, P. J. Hills, J. M. Kilty and S. O'Connell for much help and inspiration.

References

1. L. R. B. Elton, The use of duplicated lecture notes and self-tests in University teaching, *Aspects of Educational Technology* **IV**, Pitman, London 1970, p. 366.
2. J. McLeish, *The Lecture Method,* Cambridge Monographs on Teaching Methods, No. 1, Cambridge Institute of Education 1968.
3. L. R. B. Elton, P. J. Hills and S. O'Connell, *Phys. Educ.* **6**, 95 (1971).
4. D. J. Boud and S. O'Connell, *Visual Educ.,* December 1970, p. 12.
5. P. J. Hills, *Visual Educ.,* January 1971, p. 7.
6. J. M. Kilty, *Visual Educ.,* February 1971, p. 17.
7. R. M. Beard, *Small Group Discussion in University Teaching,* Department of Higher Education, University of London 1967.
8. F. S. Keller, *J. Appl. Behaviour Anal.* **1**, 79 (1968).
9. B. A. Green, Jr., *Amer. J. Phys.* **39**, 764 (1971).
10. S. O'Connell, A. W. Wilson and L. R. B. Elton, *Nature* **222**, 526 (1969).
11. L. R. B. Elton, *Concepts of Classical Mechanics,* McGraw-Hill, Maidenhead 1971.

Note added in proof:

Further experience with the Keller plan (L. R. B. Elton, D. J. Boud, J. Nuttall and B. C. Stace, *Chemistry in Britain,* April 1973) has strongly indicated that this view needs modifying. Abandoning normal lecturing has not led to a loss of group feeling; on the contrary, students in a Keller plan course give the impression of greater group cohesion. Further, since there are no lectures, the students must work actively, if any work is to be done, and this is likely to lead to a greater use of any new materials and methods provided.

CHAPTER 11

Programmed Learning Methods in Advanced Science Courses

D. E. BILLING

AIMS OF THIS CHAPTER

1. To provide basic information about programmed learning, and to extend its conception, by answering the following questions:
    - (*a*) What is programmed learning?
    - (*b*) What are the essential elements of a programmed approach?
    - (*c*) How is programmed learning related to other teaching methods?
    - (*d*) What type of material may be programmed, and at what level?
    - (*e*) What are the types of learning programme?
    - (*f*) What media may be used?
    - (*g*) How are learning programmes constructed?
    - (*h*) What are the advantages over conventional methods?
    - (*i*) What is the evidence that learning programmes are effective?
    - (*j*) What are the sources of learning programmes, and what future have they?

2. To encourage familiarity with the programmed method by giving examples from programmes on advanced science.

3. To interest science lecturers in programmed learning by revealing its potential uses.

TEST

The reader may like to use the following test, to guide him as to whether he is already familiar with the approach adopted in this chapter. The answers will be found on p. 166.

1. Which *one* of the following definitions most nearly describes a learning programme?

A.　A timetable or schedule of study periods, arranged for individual students;

B.　A printed sequence of short steps, by means of which the student learns a topic gradually in a set order, by responding to questions,

C.　A systematically designed and structured set of materials or events, through which the student achieves defined learning objectives;

D.　Subject matter presented to the student automatically, by means of a teaching machine or computer;

E.　A replacement for the lecture or other face-to-face teaching by means of individual study, perhaps using pre-recorded audio-tapes;

F.　An educational television or film programme;

G.　A sort of scrambled book, through which the student picks his way, being directed by his answers to multiple-choice questions.

2.　Which of the following features are among the essential elements of the programmed approach (choose several)?

A.　Small steps;

B.　Systematic design;

C.　Validation;

D.　Overt response to questions;

E.　Knowledge is inculcated;

F.　Objectives defined in advance;

G.　Gradual and ordered shaping of behaviour;

H.　Individual, rather than group learning.

3.　The relationship of a learning programme to a lecture is *best* described by which *one* of the following:

A.　Programmed learning supplements the lecture by providing support material for new topics, or remedial work, or revision;

B.　Programmed materials complement the lecture, and the lecture itself may be programmed;

C.　Programmed learning replaces the lecture by individual learning, leaving the lecturer free to design such materials.

4.　Which of the following media may be used in a learning programme (choose one or more)?

A.　Printed pages;

B.　Film;

C.　Television;

D.　Audio-tape;

E.　Slides, film-strip, overhead projector transparencies, or other still visual material.

THE NATURE OF PROGRAMMED LEARNING

Programmed learning is a systematic approach to providing situations and materials from which students learn effectively. It is only in the rigour of this systematic design that it differs from non-programmed teaching methods.

The components of this approach are:

(i) Specification of broad aims and more detailed objectives;
(ii) Construction of a test which will measure how far the students attain the objectives;
(iii) Design and construction of materials and situations from which the student will learn to achieve the objectives;
(iv) Validation of these materials by means of trials with students;
(v) Revision of the materials, on the basis of the trials. Several cycles of validation and revision may be necessary, before students' performances on the test are satisfactory.

Programmed learning is an *approach,* not a particular manifestation of that approach such as a teaching machine, a printed series of small steps, or a television production. The programmed approach has also been called the 'systems approach', because it utilizes 'feed-back' of information on the progress of the student (i.e. validation data) in order to modify the operation of the system (i.e. the learning materials are revised). In this sense, the programmed approach is one aspect of the curriculum development model discussed in Chap. 1.

AIMS AND OBJECTIVES

We shall use the phrase 'curriculum development model' (or sometimes 'systems approach') to refer to a whole course; the phrase 'programmed approach' may then usefully be applied to a component of such a course—a course unit.

The course will have broad aims, such as 'to encourage understanding of the inter-relationships of scientific concepts', or 'to encourage a favourable attitude to the use of scientific methodology'. For each course unit, these will be specified in more detail, as objectives (*see* Chap. 3). A useful objective is one which lists all the relevant factors in the learning situation, preferably in such a form that its achievement is measurable. If possible, we wish to specify: *who* will be able to *do what, how well,* and under *what conditions,* if the learning has been successful.

ACHIEVEMENT MEASUREMENT

The advantage of formulating such a 'behavioural' objective is that test construction is facilitated. Such an objective might be: 'final-year students, conversant with Russell-Saunders coupling for a single electron, will be able to predict correctly the ground atomic terms of all the d^n configurations, when given lists of the terms arising, but in the absence of notes or books and within a period of five minutes'. In this case, simply rewording the objective will convert it into a test item: 'Predict the correct ground terms of each of the d^n configurations, given that the terms arising are listed in the following table . . .'

Methods of assessing whether such objectives have been achieved are discussed, in more detail in Chap. 16. In some cases, the objectives may be too general, and will have to be analysed further into sub-objectives, before test items can be constructed.

When completed, such a 'criterion' test may be used after the students have studied programmed materials. This is referred to as a 'post-test'. Besides aiding the evaluation of the programme, a post-test enables the student to check his progress. If the programme is in several sections (one for each sub-objective), the sections may have their own 'diagnostic' tests.

The criterion test has a further use; if students attempt it *before* studying the programme, their results will guide them as to whether they already know its content and therefore do not need to work through the material. Each section may have its corresponding 'pre-test'. The use of pre-tests enables programmes to be designed for a specific group of students, and therefore assists the precise specification of objectives.

However, most programmes do not start from the assumption of zero knowledge or skills on the part of the student. The specification of pre-requisite knowledge or skills completes the requirements for a precise specification of the group of students at whom the programme is aimed. In the example above, we required students, at entry, to be 'conversant with Russell-Saunders Coupling for a single electron'. It is necessary to ensure that only students who do have the pre-requisite abilities actually use the programme. For the purpose of selecting such students, an 'entry test' must be devised. Thus, the students are subjected to *two* quite different tests before working through a programme; only those who pass the entry test *and* fail the pre-test will benefit properly from the programme. This group, at whom the programme is aimed, is referred to as the 'target population'. It may, of course, be necessary to write further programmes to help those students who fail the entry test. Such a series of programmes may be seen as component sections of a course; in this case, the post-test of one section might serve as the entry-test for the next section.

The interpretation of test results is simplified if it is capable of being marked objectively. The items should, therefore, be of the fixed-response or short-answer varieties (*see* Chap. 16).

PROGRAMMED MATERIALS

Having specified objectives and examined the characteristics of the 'target population', the next step is to design some learning materials to fit the specifications. In searching for guiding principles for the translation of objectives into an appropriate learning package, it is useful to examine the component parts of the objective.

What the student will do may condition the ordering within the programme. Thus, a subject with a logical structure might be best presented as a programme depending on the same *logical* order of development.

Since the student will be able to *do* things as a result of working through the programme, he must learn to *do* the *same* things in the programme. This means that the student must be *actively* involved while studying the programme. Typically he would be asked to respond to questions ('stimuli')—but the response might be covert rather than overt, if the material is conceptual. Thus, it would be quicker for the student to think the answer to a question such as 'what relationship does this graph suggest?', than for him to actually write it down. In some cases, an overt response would be demanded by the objective. Thus a programme on a manipulative skill like titration would necessitate responses in which the student actually *used* apparatus and chemicals. A programme which only taught *knowledge* of how to fill a pipette, or of how to work out the result, would be inadequate. Similarly, an objective which required the student to demonstrate that he understood Boyle's Law by *applying* it to some problems, would not be satisfactorily served by only teaching the student to *state* Boyle's Law. Besides writing, overt responses may involve drawing a diagram, solving a problem, constructing a graph or a table, or practical experiments.

What conditions obtain, in the environment in which the student will have to operate, is also an important factor. The student must learn to perform his task in the same 'operational environment' as the expert ('master performer') actually does the job. Features of the environment may make the task less or more difficult to perform, and should thus be incorporated into the learning programme. Thus, the master performer may have access to books and advice; or he may have to work in a noisy plant, with production held up while he solves a problem.

Who will learn to attain the objective, has already been discussed in terms of specification of the target population. However, there are other characteristics of people, in general, which significantly affect the construction of a programme: we must understand *how* the student learns. It is, in fact, from theories of learning that most modern programming techniques have been developed. The *psychological* structure of the topic may, therefore, have an important part to play in determining the order of treatment within the programme.

TYPES OF PROGRAMME

1. Linear Programmes

The most influential ideas have been the behavioural theories of B. F. Skinner.[1] He has shown that behaviour may be shaped by rewarding successful performances of an operation. Programmes, based upon such a learning theory, emphasize the gradual nature of the shaping, by proceeding in a sequence of steps ('frames'), directed towards the desired goal; each step is reinforced by the reward of knowing that the correct answer to question has been obtained. Skinner says that the student must only rarely fail to respond correctly to questions, or he will lose motivation. This type of programme requires the student to progress in a straight line through one sequence of frames; it is therefore called a *linear* programme. The following sequence from the beginning of a printed programme on 'Solubility' illustrates this format.[2] It also demonstrates the indirect method of posing questions, by leaving blanks to be completed, and one layout for the answers—in the right hand column. The student covers this column, and gradually works down the page, revealing one answer at a time.

Many types of format have been used for printed frames—mainly to decrease the likelihood of the student accidentally receiving the correct answer before he has responded to the question. In fact, such 'cheating' does not seem to decrease the performance of programmes—in which case possibly the making of active responses is less important than the systematic structuring of the materials. One of the better arrangements is to have only one frame per page, with answers on the reverse side; this usually results in a thick book with a small page size as with Pattison's programme[3] on 'Gas Chromatography'. The Chemical Principles programmes of Lassila *et al.*,[4] are modifications with several frames per page.

D. E. Billing

Solubility

1. When a salt (electrolyte) dissolves in water at constant temperature its ions are distributed throughout the water and solution continues until a saturated solution is given. Equilibrium has then been attained i.e. the forward and back reactions proceed at .... rates.

equal

2. Thus for silver chloride we have the equation

$$AgCl_{(s)} \rightleftharpoons Ag^+ + Cl^-$$

and we write the equilibrium in terms of K_S the solubility product.

$$K_S = [Ag^+][Cl^-]$$

Similarly for $PbCl_2$ the equation is written

$$Pb\,Cl_{2_{(s)}} \rightleftharpoons \dots\dots\dots\dots\dots\dots\dots$$

$Pb^{2+} + 2Cl^-$

3. For $Pb\,Cl_2$ $K_S = $ ....

and for $Fe(OH)_3$ $K_S = $ ....

$[Pb^{2+}][Cl^-]^2$
$[Fe^{3+}][OH^-]^3$

4. If we added KCl to a solution of silver chloride this would change the chloride ion concentration but K_S for silver chloride would be ....

unchanged

5. This solubility product concept is very useful in dealing with sparingly soluble electrolytes.

Since silver chloride has a very small solubility in water a mixture containing 0.1 M potassium chloride and saturated silver chloride would contain chloride ions at a concentration of 0.1 gm ion/l due to the potassium chloride only and a negligible amount due to the silver chloride.

Therefore if $K_S = [Ag^+][Cl^-] = 10^{-10}$ (gm ion/l)^2 and $[Cl^-] = 10^{-1}$ gm ion/l then

$$[Ag^+] = \dots\dots\dots\dots\dots \text{ gm ion/p}$$

10^{-9}

(Reprinted from D. E. Hoare[2])

A further type of layout, with answers placed between frames is illustrated in the following sequences. To follow them, cover the whole page and gradually move the cover down the page. These also demonstrate an important point—learning programmes can call for understanding, application, evaluation, deductive and inductive reasoning, on the part of the student. Thus, learning programmes do not simply 'condition' the student by 'spoon-feeding' him with the correct answers until he memorizes them—although some early programmes did this. Programmes are applicable to the higher orders of Bloom's hierarchy of cognitive objectives, as well as to the lower orders. Thus, a programme may put the student in a position where he must make a discovery in order to proceed. Such programmes might be called[5] 'heuristic', and one technique involved has been referred to as the EGRUL approach. Here, examples (EG's) of a rule are given, from which the student himself discovers the rule (RU) involved. This is unfortunately less common than the RULEG version, in which a rule is stated first, and the student then works through examples.[6] Since the range of types of abilities, required by learning programmes, varies widely, there is no restriction on the academic level for which programmes may be designed.

The first example is from a linear programme on electronegativity,[7a] which forms part of a set of seven programmes on general concepts for 'A' level or first-year university students. The student has just been asked to inspect tables of ionization energy and electron affinity, to find which is the larger quantity. In frame 23 he then recognizes the dependence of electronegativity on ionization energy. He goes on to apply what he has already deduced about the latter quantity, to make predictions concerning the periodic variation of electronegativity (frames 24-26), and in frame 27 discovers the 'diagonal relationship'. Note the use of suggested choices of answer, in frames 24-27. Such partial 'prompting' was necessary, since students otherwise found the *form* of the answer difficult to decide. However, the use of such fixed responses is less usual than constructed responses in linear programmes.

23.   Thus the trends in electronegativity usually follow those of the . . . .

First ionization energy

24.   So electronegativity will usually . . . . (increase/decrease) going from left to right in a row of the periodic table.

increase

25.   and will . . . . (increase/decrease) going down a group of the periodic table

decrease

26.   So for example Selenium is . . . . (more/less) electro-negative than Germanium, and Berylium is . . . . (more/less) electronegative than Barium.

more;   more

27.   If we move diagonally, for example from Be to Al, we would *expect* the electronegativity to . . . . (decrease/increase/remain about the same).

remain about the same—this is the 'diagonal relationship'.

The effective nuclear charge programme[7b] is also part of the set referred to above. Frame 39 allows the student to verify a relationship between ionization energy and atomic number. Frame 40 leads him to derive an equation from an earlier frame, and frame 41 asks him to apply it to the case of X-ray emission.

39.   Hence give a rough plot of I.E. against Z (not Z^*) for the isoelectronic species Li, Be^+, B^{2+}, C^{3+}

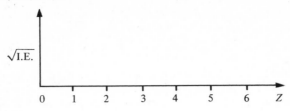

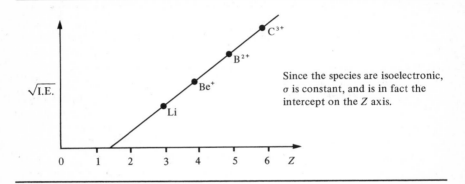

Since the species are isoelectronic, σ is constant, and is in fact the intercept on the Z axis.

40.   Another method of measuring σ and Z^* is by means of X-ray spectroscopy. By taking differences of energy levels in Frame 37 we obtain

$$h_p = \Delta E = E_1 - E_2 = \ldots\ldots\ldots\ldots\ldots$$

$$h\nu = 13.6 (Z^*)^2 \left[\frac{1}{(n_2^*)^2} - \frac{1}{(n_1^*)^2} \right] eV$$

41.   The K_α X-ray line is considered to be due to an electron falling from the second quantum shell ($n_1 = 2 = n_2^*$) to the first quantum shell ($n_2 = 1 = n_1^*$) to replace an electron ejected from there in electron bombardment of the surface. This assumes Z^* is constant during the process. To overcome this difficulty, σ is taken as 1.00, rather than 0.30 ($1s^2$) or 3.30 ($1s^1 2s^2 2p^6$). Hence, the K_α line of iron occurs at $h\nu = \Delta E = \ldots\ldots\ldots\ldots$ eV.

$$\Delta E = 13.6 \times (26 - 1)^2 \times (\frac{1}{1^2} - \frac{1}{2^2}) = 6370 \text{ eV}$$

The next frames are from a programme[7c] on Russell-Saunders Coupling, designed as an introduction to transition-metal electronic spectroscopy for final year honours degree students. In frame 6, the student evaluates a table of data and extracts from it an important principle. In frame 18, the student is asked to draw a diagram and from this he discovers a rule in frame 19. Notice that questions may be posed directly, as well as by leaving a blank space. Usually a direct question is better than an indirect question, because in the latter case the sentence does not make sense until the answer is inserted. Revised versions, involving only direct questions, have now been written for all these programmes. Naturally, the question must test the understanding or knowledge of something important and relevant to the particular frame.

6.   The magnitude of this interaction is $\zeta s_i \cdot l_i$, where ζ is the spin-orbit coupling constant for a single electron. This is measured in energy units, or usually cm^{-1} The table gives ζ for several atoms and ions. Study this and decide for which ions spin-orbit coupling is the smallest of the three interactions:

....

_____

At least as far as the end of the first row of transition metals.

_____

18.   Combine the two diagrams you gave for L and S to produce J.

_____

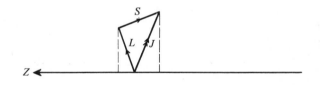

19.   Whereupon we see that $M_J = $ ....

_____

$M_J = M_L + M_S$

_____

Such programme materials are very highly structured—'tightly programmed'. However, looser programming may often be adequate, as with the study questions and comments taken from a programme on the qualitative aspects of ligand-field theory for second year honours students.[7d] In this case, the questions are placed at the end of a conventional linear programme, and ask the student to apply what he has learned to new situations.

D. E. Billing

Study Questions

8.   Would promotion of an electron to the next state make an SN_2 reaction more feasible, and does this suggest a method of calculating contributions to activation energy from crystal-field splitting energies?

Repeat this exercise for SN_2 reactions of other octahedral complexes; also for their SN_1 reactions, and for SN_2 reactions of square-planar complexes.

9.   Consider how the different charges of Cr^{2+} and Cr^{3+} ions will affect metal-ligand bond-lengths in their octahedral complexes. Apply the findings of question (6) to decide whether octahedral high-spin Cr^{2+} or Cr^{3+} complexes will be distorted. Suppose in redox reactions, Cr^{2+} lost an electron, or Cr^{3+} gained an electron. Does the Franck-Condon principle, when applied to such electronic transitions, predict that they will be easy or difficult?

Comments

In study questions 1-3, we have introduced the concept of 'crystal-field stabilization energy' (CFSE), and have applied it in the exploration of anomalies in lattice energies and heats of solvation, and in the exploration of the distribution of metal ions in octahedral or tetrahedral sites.

In study question 4, we have shown that crystal-field splitting affects measured ionic radii.

In study questions 5 and 6, we have deduced that many complexes will be distorted. Such distortions are said to result from the 'Jahn-Teller' theorem.

In study questions 7 and 8, we have shown that crystal-filled splitting affects the rate of nucleophilic substitution reactions. Some complexes will be inert, others labile.

In study question 9, we have considered the kinetics and mechanisms of another type of reaction—the electron transfer reaction.

The next two examples are taken from loosely structured programmes, which are course units 5 ('States of Matter') and 28 ('The Wave Nature of Light') of the Open University Science Foundation Course.[8] The second of these illustrates the inclusion of practical work within programmes. Practical responses have also been used in programmes by Glynn,[9] Hogg[10] and McDuffie.[11]

THE MAXWELL DISTRIBUTION

The distribution is shown graphically in Figure 6. Notice that some of the molecules have velocities appreciably higher (and lower) than the average velocity. Three per cent, for example, have velocities between 1.9 and 2.1 times the average velocity. (These velocities are represented by the area hatched in on Figure 6; the total number of molecules is represented by the total area under the curve.) Figure 7 shows the effect of temperature change on the Maxwell distribution.

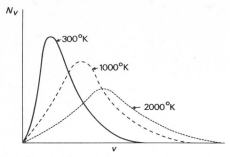

Figure 7 To show how the Maxwell distribution changes with temperature. Notice that at higher temperatures the distribution becomes broader.

Now what would happen if all three per cent of the molecules, having a velocity of about twice the average, collected at one point in the room in which you are sitting, say in the few per cent of the room volume in the neighbourhood of your head?

The temperature in the region of your head would suddenly increase (since temperature is proportional to $\bar{v^2}$) to four times the average value in the room, say from 300 K (above Absolute Zero, remember!) to 1 200 K. This would certainly, and literally, boil your head. But you know by experimental observation (and by human experience over the centuries!) that this does not happen.

James Clerk Maxwell, who worked all this out, amused himself by postulating a superhuman being, the 'Maxwell Demon', who could sit by a hole in a wall that divided a gas container into two parts, A and B, and, using a sort of microscopic dustbin lid, would allow only those molecules moving at above-average velocity to pass from side A to side B, and only those moving with below-average velocity to pass from side B to side A.

What would happen to the gas on the side A of the wall where the fast molecules were allowed to congregate?

The gas on side A of the wall would heat up compared with the gas on side B, because the average kinetic energy of the molecules on side A would increase, and the average kinetic energy of the molecules on side B would decrease.

Again, observation over the centuries shows that this sort of statistical improbability does not happen spontaneously. Scientists have generalized this experience in the Second Law of Thermodynamics.

REFRACTION

Many examples of refraction are seen in everyday life. An example which you can try for yourself is illustrated in Figure 6 (a).

NOW DO HOME EXPERIMENTS A AND B

What is the cause of the illusions you have just seen?

The 'illusions' are caused by our interpretation of the images recorded by our eyes. We naturally assume that an object lies in the direction in which we have to look in order to see it, but if there is a boundary at which refraction can occur, between our eyes and the object, then the direction of the light may be changed by refraction. Another example of this effect is that the depth of a pool of water appears less than it really is.

The way refraction causes these apparent contractions is shown in Figure 6 (b). For a similar reason, objects appear displaced when viewed at an angle through a sheet of glass or perspex (Fig. 6 (c)).

The possibility of accidental 'cheating' is reduced if the programme is not restricted to a printed format. The simplest means of doing this is found in programmed tape/slide sequences. A question is asked in the audio-tape accompanying the slide visuals, and after a pause, the audio commentary continues with the answer.[12] A similar method is shown in the example from an 'audio-tutorial'. This consists of printed handouts accompanied by an audio commentary, on cassette. The question is posed in either medium (as here in the printed notes), and answered on the cassette. The example is taken from a series of thirteen programmes on metal complexes,[13] for second and final year honours students.

Substitution Reaction Mechanisms

Consider now an octahedral low-spin d^6 complex such as most of those of Co (III).

What is the electronic configuration, in terms of occupancy of t_{2g} and e_g energy levels?

Will these electrons therefore repel the incoming X ligand to the same extent as the Y ligands already present (bearing in mind the orientation of e_g and t_{2g} relative to M-X and M-Y bonds)?

Are there any correctly oriented orbitals which could accept electrons from the incoming X ligand so as to form a bond? Considering both of these effects, has the incoming X ligand as much chance to form a bond as the Y ligands already present?

What other configurations will behave in a similar way? What configurations will behave differently?

Another way to prevent 'cheating' is to use a teaching machine; this is an automatic way of presenting one frame or one answer at a time—using a filmstrip projector, advanced by pushing buttons. For linear programmes, the teaching machine behaves simply as an expensive page-turning device, and its use is usually unwarranted.

A further way of preventing 'cheating' is not to give an answer to the question. Usually, however, the student needs 'immediate knowledge of results' (KR) in order to confirm his progress. The omission of an answer is justified only for questions which pose convergent problems, so that the student will, himself know when he has the correct answer.

Summarizing, the essential features of learning programmes are:
(*a*)   An ordered sequence of stimulus items (frames);
(*b*)   Student response to specific questions;
(*c*)   Gradual shaping of behaviour;
(*d*)   Systematic design;
(*e*)   Objectives defined in advance;
(*f*)   Validation;
(*g*)   Entry tests and Pre-tests;
(*h*)   Post-test.
In addition, the essential characteristics of the linear format are:
(*a*)   One sequence of frames (only);
(*b*)   Behavioural approach;
(*c*)   Minimal errors.

At various times, the following have been claimed as essential to learning programmes:

(*a*)   Knowledge is inculcated rather than thought encouraged;
(*b*)   Small steps;
(*c*)   The teacher is replaced;
(*d*)   Individual rather than group learning;
(*e*)   One style of programming, only, can be used in one programme;
(*f*)   Immediate knowledge of results;
(*g*)   Overt responses;
(*h*)   Order of treatment same as logical order of subject;
(*i*)   Printed pages or teaching machine as the medium;
(*j*)   Use of prompts;
(*k*)   Self-pacing.

More recent experience[14,15] has shown that none of these are essential. Some of the reasons will be given when examining other programming modes; some have already been given. Thus, all media are usable; parts of this chapter have been presented as a programmed lecture,[16] while programmed television productions have been made.[17] In such cases, self-pacing is impossible, but studies have shown[18] that group learning is no less efficient than individual learning. The programmed approach does not dispense with the teacher, but the teaching method adopted depends on the objectives and any constraints; a lecture may therefore be part of a programmed course unit.

Besides the essential characteristics, linear programmes often have the following inessential features:

(*a*)   Small steps;
(*b*)   Constructed responses;
(*c*)   Use of prompts.

Prompts are one means of achieving minimal errors. There are two main types: formal and thematic. This is a f - - - - l prompt. The thematic prompt indicates not the *form* of the response, but what the context is—what sort of theme it is about. The sequence prompt is a variation upon the _____ *prompt; it also gains its force from the context. Thus it may refer to material learned in the previous few frames. Sequence prompts are a valuable way of linking the concepts of one frame with those of the next, so as to emphasize the structure of the subject in a coherent manner.[5] In many early programmes which just attempted to inculcate facts, very long series of similar frames were used. Each contained a prompt, but the strength of the prompt faded until the last frame in the series ('terminal frame') contained no prompts. In some frames, the strength of the prompts was so high that the student was, in effect, being asked merely to copy some words in order to give his response.

2.   Branching Programmes

The linear programme would be adequate if all students had the same ability, motivation and pace of learning. However, this is unlikely, and therefore to produce minimal errors for all students, the programme must proceed at such a slow pace that the quick

---

* answer: thematic.

learner may become bored. There is another type of programme, in which a modification is introduced to provide for such mixed learning speeds (illustrated here by part of a programme on programmes[16]).

---

1. Consider how this could best be done? (Select *one* answer)
    A. by pacing the programme to suit average students;
    B. by introducing branches to cater for various speeds;
    C. by telling the faster students to skip frames at their discretion;
    D. by telling the slower students to re-read the programme.

Directions: If you chose A, go to frame 2a
            If you chose B, go to frame 2b
            If you chose C, go to frame 2c
            If you chose D, go to frame 2d

2a. A programme paced to suit only the average students would be unsatisfactory for the majority of others. There is a device which will direct the efforts of students of several ability ranges more satisfactorily. Return to frame 1, and try again.

2b. The provision of branches would indeed suit students of several ranges of learning speed. This *is* the best method, although it can only cater for a finite number of speeds. (Go on now to the next part of this chapter.)

2c. If the students could skip frames at their discretion, they might miss frames which they actually needed. Further, they might not get necessary reinforcement. Instead, we could construct a main series of frames for fast students, putting a question after each frame. On the basis of their answers to these questions, the students would then be directed from the main 'trunk' of the programme into several _____.

Branches

(Go on now to the next part of this chapter)

2d. Re-reading the programme might encourage a better performance the second or the tenth time. Would the student necessarily understand what gave him difficulty before? Would he have obtained remedial help to sort out conceptual difficulties?

No, he may understand no more the second time; he may only have memorized the correct responses.
(Go to frame 2e)

2e. Further, the student is being given negative reinforcement—avoidance of the 'punishment' of having to read the programme yet again. Positive reinforcement ('reward') has been proved to be a superior technique.

Negative reinforcement may lead to the student's loosing confidence and motivation. Which of the following methods would avoid this problem in the more satisfactory manner? (Select *one* answer):
    A. Each student follows a 'branch' or remedial loop and does not know the length or content of other branches;

B.   All students follow exactly the same sequences of frames, irrespective of their difficulties.

Your answer:
   If A, then go to the next part of the chapter;
   If B, then go to frame 2f.

2f.   Was not this the situation we were trying to modify in frame 1? Go back to frame 1 and try again.

Branching programmes were first used by Crowder.[19] In such learning materials, decisions about individual routes are made *internally* by the student; branching programmes are therefore sometimes called 'intrinsic', to distinguish them from linear programmes in which the student's route is determined 'extrinsically' by the programme designer. The usual means of restricting the number of branches to manageable proportions is to give the student a selection of fixed-responses. Multiple choice responses are therefore a common characteristic of branching programmes. However, they are not an essential feature; the student can be asked to construct a response, and then to compare his effort with a multiple-choice selection of answers.[20] It is also possible to let the student decide his route, on the basis of the confidence he has in his understanding of the material. Remedial loops are ideally designed to cater for common misconceptions.

The linear programme uses student responses as a device to ensure active learning; whereas the branching programme uses responses as a means of directing the student into an appropriate branch. In fact, Skinner (although not the writers of loosely structured programmes) says that the student must actively respond to *all* the material in each frame; his steps are therefore short. Crowder says that the main factor producing learning is not active response, but simply the exposure to the text; his steps may therefore be quite long.

Just as in a heuristic linear programme, the emphasis in a branching programme is often upon the student's *discovering* an answer to a question, rather than his receiving training to respond in the way he has been told is correct. In this sense, the student perceives the whole problem at once, and needs a flash of insight to solve it. Branching programmes are closely related to the 'Gestalt' (German: whole form) school of learning theory, which stresses insight via an appreciation of the shape of the problem.

The only essential features of branching programmes are the emphasis on individual learning (self-pacing) and the inclusion of parallel series of frames or remedial loops (in addition to the essential features of all learning programmes).

The following inessential characteristics are commonly found in branching programmes:
   (*a*)   Large steps;
   (*b*)   Multiple-choice responses;
   (*c*)   Explanation of incorrect answers;
   (*d*)   Gestalt view of problem-solving.

Most teaching machines utilize branching programmes (linear programmes do not need such mechanization); however, branching programmes are rarely written only for teaching machines.

The example[21] comes from *Programmed Problems in Thermodynamics*.

3a.1 An ideal gas is taken from the state $P = 100$, $v = 1$ to the state $P = 4$, $v = 5$ by two different quasi-static processes. The units are arbitrary.

Process (a) is described by the equation

$$P = 100/v^2 \qquad (1)$$

while process (b) is described, within our range of the variables, by

$$P = 124 - 24v \qquad (2)$$

The two processes are shown on a P–v diagram in Fig. 1.

What is the work done per mole in each process?
Compare your answer with that on frame 3a.3.
If you need help, turn to 3a.2.

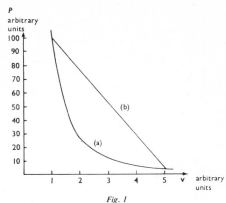

Fig. 1

3a.2 Write down the definition of work for a chemical system and use equations (1) and (2) to make suitable substitutions in this definition.

Complete the problem and turn to 3a.3.

3a.3

Process (a) $w = \int_i^f P \, dv = 100 \int_1^5 \frac{dv}{v^2} = 80$

Process (b) $w = \int_i^f P \, dv = 124 \int_1^5 dv - 24 \int_1^5 v \, dv = 208$

Is the work done on or by the gas?
Turn to 3a.4.

(Reprinted from E. Braun and E. T. Wait[21].)

3.   Hybrid Programmes

Purists, of either the linear or the branching ideologies would argue that these two approaches should not be mixed. However, more flexible attitudes now prevail,[20] and all programming modes are mixed, as appropriate. Programmers are now designing their materials to suit the particular task, rather than to reflect a particular model of the learning process. The only requirement, excluding constraints on time and cost, is that the final programme should work; this will be ensured by the validation procedure.

An example is given of a programme on alcohols at 'A'-level.[9] This is mainly linear (involving practical work), but includes some branches.

D10

Action of sodium on propan-1-ol, propan-2-ol, butan-1-ol, and butan-2-ol

Practical work

Caution
See B1 for instructions about handling sodium.

Place 2 cm³ of propan-1-ol, propan-2-ol, butan-1-ol, and butan-2-ol
into separate dry test-tubes (or small beakers). Add to each a piece of
sodium (about the size of a *small* pea).

Question

Arrange each of the following pairs in order of vigour of reaction with
sodium:
a. propan-1-ol and propan-2-ol
b. butan-1-ol and butan-2-ol. (See D9 for formulae.)

 D11

D11

Action of dilute permanganate solution on butan-1-ol and butan-2-ol

Practical work

Treat 2 cm³ samples of butan-1-ol and butan-2-ol with 2–4 drops of
dilute (0.01M) permanganate solution. Add 2 cm³ of acetone to each
sample of alcohol to increase miscibility (see D6).

Question

Which alcohol is oxidized more rapidly?

 D12 if you wish to investigate the action of dichromate solution and of
sulphuric acid on propan-1-ol and propan-2-ol; otherwise D13.

4. Adaptive Teaching Machines

If the range of abilities of students is very wide, the number of branches required may
be very great. Another approach is to provide the student with learning materials
which exactly match his ability—as shown by his rate of making errors as the programme proceeds. Such a programme therefore adapts to the student. Controlling the
programme and checking the student's progress then requires a sophisticated
machine—the adaptive teaching machine introduced by G. Pask.[22] One means of
controlling the learning situation is to use a computer as the teaching machine. Much
work on Computer Based Learning (sometimes called Computer Assisted Instruction—
C.A.I.) has been done,[23] particularly in the U.S.A. The high cost and lack of

appropriate visual material (apart from teletype output) for the student, are usual difficulties with this approach. Chap. 12 describes some British work.

Another type of teaching machine is the simulator. In cases where manipulative skills must be learned without the high cost of making errors with the real equipment, the relevant aspects of the real situation may be simulated. Thus, pilots may learn to fly on a simulator, without endangering lives and property. The machine presents the consequences of all of his actions to the student, using the same senses (vision, hearing, touch etc.) he would be using in the real situation.

When the subject involves the interplay of personalities and decisions in a group, role-playing is a useful form of simulation. The group acts as a teaching machine. One method of provoking such group interactions is for the group to make a case-study— examining (perhaps by role-playing) how decisions were made in a real situation.

5.   Structural Communications

The structural communication is a form of branching programme, in which a few very large multiple-completion questions are used.[24] The answers to the multiple comple- tion questions are chosen from a table known as the 'Response Array'. A number of questions may be asked about the same response array; these questions test the comprehension of fairly lengthy sections of text which precede them. According to his selections of answers, the student is branched to a number of comments for guidance. The example[25] is taken from a structural communication on the phase rule.

Problems

Think carefully about these problems before selecting the responses which you think are most relevant.

1. Figure 8 shows a phase diagram for carbon dioxide, in which pressure is plotted against temperature. It is well known that at a pressure around atmospheric, solid CO_2 sublimes directly to the gas, without passing through the liquid state. This should be obvious from the figure. What are the limits of existence of the liquid phase?

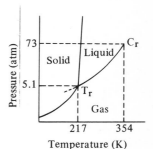

Fig. 8. CO_2 Phase Diagram.

2. The critical point of a gas is not as sharply defined as might be commonly supposed from text books. Thus the temperature at which the meniscus disappears on heating is not the same as that at which it reappears on cooling. What features of phase diagrams would you make use of in the accurate determination of the critical data of a pure substance?

3. Diamonds can be produced commercially by crystal- lization of carbon from solution in molten iron. What factors must be considered when accounting for the formation of diamonds in this way? (The phase diagram of carbon is given in Fig. 9 to help you.)

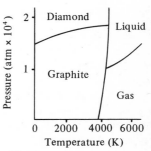

Fig. 9.

4. Helium is a unique substance in that the liquid can exist in two distinct phases which do not mix, rather like allotropic forms of solids. There is no latent heat for the phase change from one liquid phase to the other. The phase diagram is shown in Fig. 10. What features does the helium system *not* show which are common to other one-component systems?

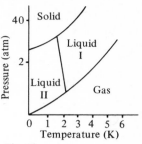

Fig. 10.

Response Matrix

1.	2.	3.	4.
A decrease of volume accompanies the phase change when heat is supplied.	All liquids show a sharp surface.	An increase in entropy accompanies the phase change when heat is supplied.	The latent heat of the phase change is zero under certain conditions.
5.	6.	7.	8.
The supercooled liquid is in a meta-stable state.	Liquids expand as they are heated.	Solid, liquid and vapour coexist in stable equilibrium at the triple point.	The pressure-volume phase diagram must be accurately plotted.
9.	10.	11.	12.
A solid-gas equilib-rium can exist above the triple point.	The rate of the phase change is very slow indeed.	There is a change of slope of the vapour pressure curve at the triple point.	At the critical point, liquid and vapour become indistinguishable.
13.	14.	15.	16.
The triple point lies at a pressure above atmospheric.	Gases become more dense as they are heated, or as they are compressed.	The rectilinear diameter of the density-pressure plot ends at the critical density.	For a pure substance, only three phases can coexist in stable equilibrium.
17.	18.	19.	20.
A substance may be denser when in the gaseous phase than when liquid.	The super-cooled liquid has a vapour pressure curve which is continuous with that of the liquid phase.	The rate of a phase change rises with rise of temperature.	Different allotropic forms exist in stable equilibrium along a line in the diagram.

The response indicator may also be used as a method of assessment. The Open University Science Foundation Course has used[8] forty-nine choice multiple comple-tion questions in such a form (*see* Chap. 16).

6.   Algorithms

When a subject has a clear pattern of decisions such as fault-tracing, these may be represented diagrammatically on a 'decision tree'. Such a diagram is known as an algorithm. It has similarities to the flow-chart used in computer programming. The example[26] shows the decisions which must be taken in arriving at a classification of the point group of a molecule (Fig. 11.1).

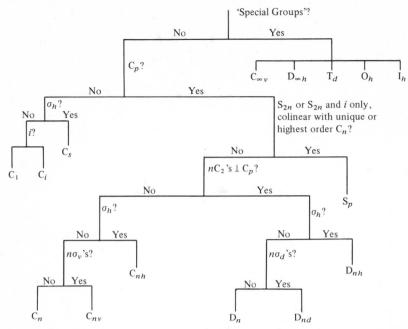

Fig. 11.1 A flow chart for classifying molecular symmetry into point groups. (From M. M. Orchin and H. H. Jaffé[26])

Algorithms are not usually meant to be learned, but to be referred to when necessary. After constant use, the expert usually does not depend on the algorithm. Qualitative Chemical Analysis tables are good examples of algorithms.

7.   Mathetics

T. Gilbert[27] developed an approach which he called 'mathetics' (Greek: learning). The method involves a detailed analysis of the desired behaviour (that of the expert), in terms of chains of stimuli and responses. This behavioural analysis is represented as a hierarchy of stimuli (S) and responses (R), rather similar to Gagné's approach.[28] However, Gagné concentrated on how the *learner* approached the topic, whereas an 'initial prescription' is made by Gilbert on the basis of the *expert's* performance— further analyses then lead to a 'teaching prescription'. Task analysis is a related method.

Gilbert identified three types of behaviour: chains, discriminations and generalizations. The latter two occur where chains join. Figure 11.2 shows examples of each of these elements.

this, the logical order of the subject is reversed for the purpose of learning; the psychological structure is emphasized. This approach may be useful when learning a skill, such as the interpretation of spectra, or the operation of an instrument. Mathias[29] has constructed a programme dealing with the interpretation of infra-red spectra in this way. The first thing the student learns is how to interpret the information about functional groups which a table of assignments (made for him) gives.

Chaining – titration of a solution

S —— R • S —— R • S —— R • S —— R • S —— R • S —— R • S —— R • S —— R • S —— R

| Solution for analysis | clean apparatus | apparatus clean | wash and fill burette with standard solution | filled | pipette unknown into flask and add indicator | colour appears | read burette and record | recorded | add standard slowly, watching colour and shaking | colour change | read burette and calculate |

Discrimination – qualitative analysis

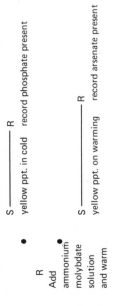

S —— R   yellow ppt. in cold   record phosphate present

• Add ammonium molybdate solution and warm

S —— R   yellow ppt. on warming   record arsenate present

Generalization – use of instruments

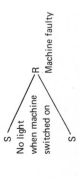

S   No light when machine switched on

R   Machine faulty

S   Pen does not move

Fig. 11.2 Components of Behavioural Analysis

The advantage of backward chaining is that the student always receives the reinforcement of completing the problem. He learns first the last step in the operation, next he tackles the penultimate step, following through the final step again for practice, gradually he works forward until he can perform the whole operation. Learning to swim is a good example of this process—the first thing learned is gliding to the edge of the pool from a yard away, and this is the last act the proficient swimmer does in crossing the pool.

Gilbert favours the shortest possible programme, so his steps are as large as the student can manage. He also recommends covert responding, to save time and effort.

8.   Adjunct Programmes

Pressey[30] thought that a test by itself was good learning material. He developed a very early form of programme on the basis of Thorndike's theories of learning according to which response is more likely if its results are rewarding—'law of effect'. The student was merely presented with a set of multiple-choice questions printed on a sheet of paper. Each possible answer had a corresponding circle in the margin; the sheet of paper was placed on a board ('key') which had holes drilled under the circles appropriate to the correct answers. The student pressed his pencil in the circles he thought corresponded to the correct answers; if he was correct, a hole appeared, and if not he tried again. Such devices are not strictly programmes, and have been called 'adjunct programmes'. Modern versions of the Pressey board use an electrical contact and a light, instead of the pencil and hole.

This work was the forerunner of self-assessment questions and the feed-back class-room; the function is to provide diagnostic information about the progress of the student, either to himself (cf. the Open University Science Foundation Course Unit[8] —Chap. 16), or to his teacher during a class.[31] A further development was the introduction of reasons why an answer was correct or incorrect.

PROGRAMME CONSTRUCTION

The steps involved in constructing a learning programme are now summarized:

1.   Consideration of the aims of the course, and specification of objectives for the course unit;

. 2.   Construction of a criterion test which will measure the extent to which *all* the objectives are achieved;

3.   Consideration of the students who will be learning, and description of their knowledge, skills, interests, aims, attitudes, emotional and personality factors; design of a suitable entry test;

4.   Analysis of objectives into sub-objectives; construction of test items to be used in the diagnostic test for any section built around an objective and its component sub-objectives;

5.   Placing the sub-objectives in an appropriate order of development, to form the skeleton of the programme;

6.   Conversion of each sub-objective into a 'terminal frame', and at the same time choosing the *medium* for the achievement of each sub-objective,

7.   Specification of the characteristics of a series of 'teaching frames', leading up to each terminal frame. The programming mode, and teaching *method* (or learning activity) must be chosen;

8.   Actual construction of the frames required by this analysis, for each section;

9.   Linking together the sections, tests and appropriate summaries, to form the first draft of the programme;

10.   Trials with the programme in order to validate it;

11.   Revision of the programme on the basis of the trials.

Most of these steps have been discussed earlier, and comments are offered here only on some of the stages.

Indications of relevant sub-objectives may often be obtained by examining in detail the implications of the nouns and verbs in the statement of the objective itself. Thus, one objective in a programme on volumetric analysis might be: 'The student will be able to *calibrate* a *grade A pipette (25 cm³)* at the *ambient temperature* and to ± *0·2 per cent accuracy*, using *normal laboratory facilities*'. Some relevant sub-objectives would then be: recognizing a pipette of the correct volume and grade; cleaning, filling and emptying it; weighing water; measuring temperature; looking up the density of water; appreciation of the need for accuracy and ways of obtaining it; appreciation of the need to repeat to obtain a mean result; working out the results (including estimation of error); knowledge of normal laboratory facilities; knowledge of the calibration procedure. Performance of many of these sub-objectives would usually be assumed to be amongst the students' initial abilities. Some sub-objectives would need even further analysis, to yield a complicated hierarchy of sub-objectives—each of which must be attained before the objective itself is within reach. Thus, the operation of filling a pipette requires the skills to suck, to manipulate the finger on the end of the pipette, to position the meniscus correctly, and to remove the clinging drop. The correct positioning of the meniscus involves knowledge, an attitude (favourable to doing it correctly) and possibly understanding, as well as a practical skill.

Several schemes have been suggested to aid the arranging of sub-objectives:[32]

(*a*)   Pragmatic uses of the logical and psychological structure of the topic. These might be based upon the studies, by Piaget and others,[33] of conceptual development;

(*b*)   Spiral programming, so that the same topic is covered several times (at intervals) with increasing sophistication.[34]

(*c*)   For branching programmes, the construction of a flow diagram may help—as with a computer programme;

(*d*)   Gagné analysed the skills necessary for the learner to approach the topic. This was represented as a learning hierarchy, or chain of stimuli and responses,

(*e*)   Gilbert's mathetical methods also rely upon analysing the skills necessary to perform the desired operation, and representation of these in S-R notation. However, unlike Gagné, Gilbert concentrated on the behaviour of the expert rather than the learner;

(*f*)   Mechner[35] divided each topic into 5-20 headings, written on cards. Each heading was then divided and further sub-divided several times; the levels of sub-division were indicated by using different coloured cards. The smallest 'atoms' (sub-objectives) were arranged along one axis of a matrix, frame numbers appearing along the other axis; a dot was placed in the matrix for each frame which used the term or concept referred to in each sub-objective. Thus, Mechner's learning hierarchy depends on the structure of the *subject,* whereas Gagné's is based upon the *abilities* which are necessary to learn an operation.

(*g*)   The RULEG method[6] involves ordering both rules (RU's) and appropriate examples (EG's), using matrices as aids. The 'rules' correspond to sub-objectives; their inter-relationships (similarities, differences, discriminations, generalizations and confusions) are indicated in the matrix, which lists rules along both axes.

(*h*)   The R.A.F. School of Education system[36] is a variation on the RULEG approach, in which associations and discriminations are the only relationships entered on the RU matrix—usually by different colours. The rules are numbered along the leading diagonal ('definition line') and symmetric patterns of colour appear on both sides of this. The definition line should be continuously flanked by colour; any breaks, where adjacent rules are not related in any way, may sometimes be rectified by altering the order, or by adding or replacing some rules.

CHOICE OF MEDIUM, METHOD AND MODE

An algorithm has been given by Romizowski[37] to aid the selection of media. A modified version of this appears in Fig. 11.3. The choice of the appropriate programming mode (linear, branching etc.), may be made using the algorithm given in Fig. 11.4.

These decisions interact with each other. Thus, a cine film or television production are unsuitable for branching programmes. Further choices of learning method (i.e. situation) are necessary, and are usually determined by the choices of medium and mode. Thus, a branching programme is unsuitable for the lecture or small-group method, and only works in individual learning situations. However, the method may be of over-riding importance when the objectives or constraints are considered. In this case, earlier decisions on medium and mode might have to be reconsidered. The objective 'ability to work as a member of a team' cannot be attained by individual learning methods. Similarly, the project method might be most appropriate if the objective is 'ability to demonstrate and develop initiative'. In reality, decisions on medium, mode and method would be taken simultaneously. This applies to many of the decisions in constructing a programme; the task is in practice simpler than the forbidding list of stages indicates.

Pragmatic methods are necessary in constructing the frames, although various writers have given hints[15,20,32,38,39] and illustrations have been given earlier in this chapter. The stimulus questions themselves should avoid the faults outlined in the chapter on objective testing. The formats available for linear frames have been discussed earlier. In printed branching programmes, the questions following each frame usually direct the student to other pages of the 'scrambled book'.

The trials of the programme should take place in the correct conditions, with appropriate students. However, it is often helpful to show the programme to one's colleagues as a first step, and then perhaps to see a few students, before trials on a larger scale. Data should be collected on pre-, post- and entry test results (and also section diagnostic tests, if included), item errors (linear programmes), item error rate, use of branches, and students' attitudes to the programme. Blake[40] has listed a number of methods of testing programmes.

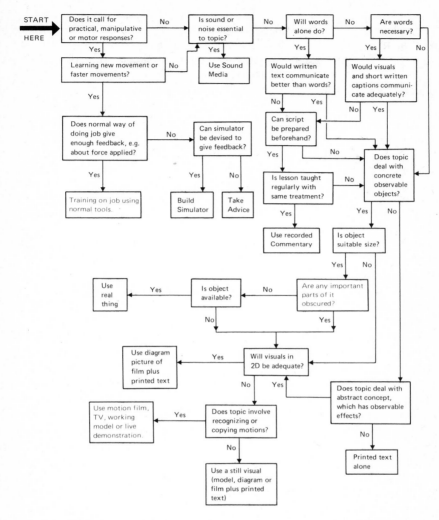

Fig. 11.3 An Algorithm for selecting learning medium. (Modified from Romizowski[37])

There are no general rules about how to revise programmes. Often a list of frames answered wrongly gives specific clues about faults in linear programmes. Branching programmes do not yield this data. Kay *et al.*[41] have given an algorithm for identifying faults in programmes.

ADVANTAGES AND DISADVANTAGES OF LEARNING PROGRAMMES[42]

1.   Programmes are self-adjusting, due to the validation procedure. This stems from the conception of programming as a systematic approach, not tied to particular

D. E. Billing

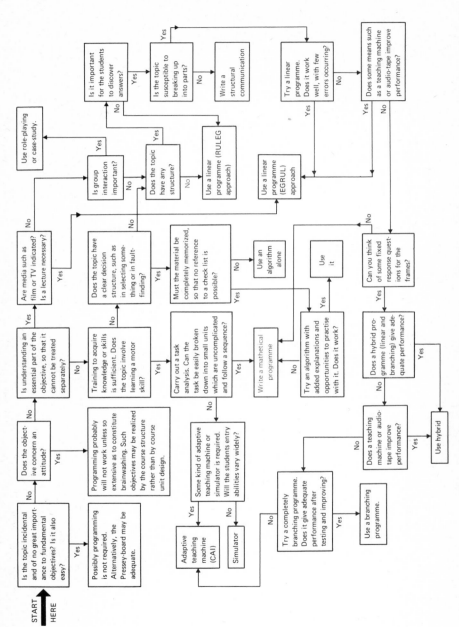

Fig. 11.4 A decision flow-chart for selecting the programme mode.

media, modes or types of learning activity; achieving given objectives is the only important factor. However, some objectives cannot be defined sufficiently precisely to enable programming; for example, 'to encourage creativity'.

2.   The systematic approach takes considerable time and effort to apply properly; it is therefore not worth programming rapidly changing, easy, peripheral or well treated topics for a few students. It would seem that constraints of time and cost should influence the objectives of the programme.

3.   The subject is broken up into manageable sections, and the approach is therefore well suited to structured topics.

4.   If the sections are small, learning is made unchallenging and students may attain the objectives without real comprehension. However, this is only true if understanding is not among the objectives, and if we ignore Gilbert's advice to make the steps as large as the students can manage.

5.   Each student can proceed at his own pace, if individual learning is permitted by the chosen medium. However, the wide variation in times which students take to complete programmes, makes rigid timetabling of such work undesirable.

6.   The student may misjudge what is his own pace, and, for this reason, possibly group learning is preferable to individual learning. Results seem to indicate that there is no reduction in performance when a student works through a programme at a predetermined rate, rather than at his own pace.

7.   Students can study in the absence of tutors, if they are so motivated. If not, this factor should be part of the target population characteristics which influence the form of the programme, and the learning situation adopted.

8.   Programmes can be used for revision purposes (although their format makes use for reference purposes difficult) and for remedial work. Good linear programmes, however, enable about 90 per cent of students to make 90 per cent of the responses correctly; the facility index is thus about 0·85, which is considerably in excess of facility indices normally found in examinations. Thus, the student's success with a learning programme may give him misplaced confidence. This should not be the case if the difference between tests of mastery and ranking tests is familiar to the student through frequent use of both types in a non-examination context.

9.   Tightly structured programmes leave the student little room for initiative, and the teacher little scope for flexibility in integrating programmes into his course.

10.   The requirement of validation means finding willing groups of students to try programmes which, since they are preliminary drafts, may lead to little or inaccurate learning. However, this is not really a disadvantage of learning programmes; all learning materials, courses and activities suffer from this problem, although it is rarely recognized.

11.   The provision for individual study enables students to make errors without being socially embarrassed, and also ensures that students do not miss instruction due to absence.

12.   High retention of learning, and fast learning are sometimes claimed for programmes. Such results depend on the programme and on the design of the experiment which establishes the claim.

13.   The students are actively involved, which promotes concentration and interest; they also usually receive immediate correction of their errors. However, these

are better seen as common characteristics of programmes, and are only advantages if they lead to better performance, or a lasting interest.

14.   At the end of the programme, we know precisely what the student is capable of doing.

THE EFFECTIVENESS OF LEARNING PROGRAMMES

In this section we consider learning programmes from the outmoded viewpoint that they are the actual *materials* (booklets etc.) which have been programmed, rather than the examples of the programmed approach—there is no research on the latter aspect.

The literature on comparisons of learning programmes with lectures is extensive, and has been reviewed several times.[14,15,32] Thus, Hartley surveyed[50] fifty-six studies (covering science and non-science subjects) involving 5,000 students. Table 11.1 shows his summary. This is classified according to whether the group using programmes were better than, equal to or worse than control groups using lectures. The overall conclusion is that programmes are better, but the extent of their superiority depends on what is used as a criterion. Three criteria are given in the Table: whether immediate retention of knowledge is achieved, whether this knowledge is retained over a period of time, and whether the time taken to learn the material is reasonably short.

Table 11.1. Effectiveness of Learning Programmes (From Hartley[50])

Measure taken	Number of Studies	Number in which programme group is:		
		Better	Equal	Worse
Immediate retention	54	35	17	2
Long-term retention	10	5	4	1
Learning time	26	24	1	1

The results obviously depend on the design of the experiment. Annett considers[45] that most of the comparisons have been fair—using the best available teacher for the control group. In some cases, the programmer himself has lectured to the control group; in these cases the control group has often performed as well or better than the programmed group. This emphasizes the point made earlier, that the important feature of the learning programme is that it forces the writer to analyse the structure of his topic, the reasons for teaching it, the order of treatment, and the important aspects; having carried out that exercise, the research data suggests that it is immaterial whether a lecture or a programme is used to present the topic.

The methodology of several of these studies can be criticized on the following grounds:

1.   Programmed learning is novel at present, and this leads to spuriously good results with programmed groups. The novelty engenders interest and therefore obscures many unsatisfactory features of programmes. It is impossible to remove this

artifact, unless the students are very familiar with programmes and lectures. While this hinders research, the novelty effect many at the same time be harnessed to improve learning.

2. The type of questions asked in post-tests, may be more familiar to the programmed group, since they have experienced them in the frames of the programme.

3. It has been suggested that merely taking the pre-test enhances the post-test results.[51] Thus, both the programmed and control groups should take the pre-test. However, Hartley *et al.*[52] found no significant effect due to pre-tests.

4. The assumption in all the studies is that programmed learning is synonymous with programmed materials using particular media (printed or teaching machines). A more important question would be 'Is a learning programme in a particular medium a better way of presenting a given topic that is a less systematically designed lecture?' The answer to this question is likely to depend greatly on the topic (its difficulty, structured nature, etc.), and on the chosen medium.

5. The studies ignore the cost in time and materials involved in programming. Thus, if a lecture and a programme are just as effective, the lecture should be chosen if it is less expensive or requires less effort.

6. The most fundamental criticism is that the studies ignore the presently accepted meaning of 'programmed learning'. Programming is an *approach* which may be applied equally to a lecture or to a booklet meant for individual study. We take a 'programmed lecture' to differ from an ordinary one in the rigour of the planning. It is therefore meaningless to conclude anything about the effectiveness of programming from comparisons of learning methods each of which may be programmed. The usefulness of such studies is extremely limited; they show whether, for a given topic, presentation in a lecture or through individual study is the better—the conclusion is expected to depend on the topic.

Further, even these comparisons only have value if both methods *are* programmed. Nothing can be concluded from the comparison of a programmed booklet with an unprogrammed lecture. The only valid comparisons are:

(*a*)   programmed method A (e.g. individual study) *vs* programmed method B (e.g. lecture);

(*b*)   programmed method A (e.g. individual study) *vs* unprogrammed method A.

(*c*)   comparisons of medium, mode, response type, step size (and other programme variables) for a given topic and a given (programmed) learning method.

In all cases, the conclusions are expected to vary with the topic, objectives, type of students, and constraints.

7. The programmed approach is self-adjusting. Thus, what the studies do not establish is whether the effort of systematically designing materials and activities actually does produce significantly better results than more intuitive approaches. The results are expected to be no worse, unless the feedback in the system is positive rather than negative—i.e. the adjustments introduced in revising a programme (based on validation data) actually produce a worse programme rather than a better one. However, what will count as 'significantly better', so as to justify the time, effort and cost involved in systematic design? Criteria must be chosen to answer this question, before it is worth carrying out further research on the effectiveness of programming.

There have been several studies of 6c. Schramm's survey found little significant difference between the effectiveness of fixed-response or constructed-response questions, small or large steps, provision or absence of knowledge of results, branching or linear texts, and machines or programmed texts.[46] Duncan & Gilbert found no significant difference between three versions of the same history programme, on the basis of immediate retention, long term retention, or students attitude to the programmes.[53] The versions were: branching, linear (branching programme without branches—i.e. the prime path), and continuous text (questions and branches omitted). The continuous text was superior to the prime path, which in turn was superior to the branching version, on the basis of learning time. The branching programme, however, better compensated for low intelligence than the linear or continuous versions.

Biran[54] obtained similar results, and also found that sixth-form and adult students preferred a straightforward presentation.

Newton & Hickey[55] varied the order of treatment in an economics programme. They found that learning was faster and performance better when sub-concepts were learned together (with their integrating concept) rather than separately.

Most workers have found no significant differences in performance between students who study programmed materials individually or in groups.

Hoare & Revans[56] have shown for chemistry undergraduates that programmes can achieve higher objectives than merely ability to recall knowledge. Comprehension and application abilities may also be learned, although the learning of knowledge was the most efficient.

Hogg[57] has studied student attitudes to programmed learning, covering a large number of chemistry programmes in several institutions of higher education. A wide selection of students have a high opinion of programmed learning. The technique is equally acceptable to students of different ability ranges, and more programmes would be used if they were available. The existing programmes have an acceptable level of difficulty, and are moderately interesting.

There appears to be a correlation between degree of interest and the opinion on usefulness of the programme. Students prefer to use programmed learning for private study to consolidate difficult material, or for revision. Using programmed learning to introduce new material was not so popular, and in particular the use in some types of supervised exercise class gained little favour. However, this study can be critized, because the questionnaire asked for comments about particular programmes and did not cater for the possibility that a student had worked through several programmes about which his opinions differed. Further, the students were not asked whether the programmes *had* been used for specific purposes (e.g. introducing new material) before giving their opinions about what programmes *could* be used for. In the present stage of acceptance in higher education very few programmes are used to introduce new material.

Leith suggests[58] that students with different types of personality may need different types of programme.

Summarizing, it is likely to be most worthwhile programming a topic which is difficult, structured, important to the course, unlikely to change, and is poorly covered in existing texts; and for situations where teachers are scarce and students numerous and of mixed prior experience; and for courses which will be used many times. These are the most favourable set of circumstances which we can imagine. In more realistic cases, we must weigh the extra value from the systems approach against the time and effort required, in order to decide whether to programme a course unit.

INFORMATION ABOUT LEARNING PROGRAMMES

A.   Literature about programming:

Kay *et al.*[41] give a good general introduction to the topic, while the practical aspects are well treated in books by Leith,[32] Pipe,[39] Brethower,[59] Romiszowski,[38] Rowntree[38] and Markle.[20] The book by Markle is particularly refreshing due to its undogmatic attitude.

Reviews of recent progress are given by Leith[14,15,32,43] and Peel.[47] Research results are surveyed by Beard,[49] Beard *et al.*,[48] Leith,[14,15,30,43] Flood Page[44] and Annett.[45]

Useful collections of papers are given in the books edited by Stones,[60] Austwick,[61] Smith *et al.*,[62] Glazer,[63] and the various volumes of *Aspects of Educational Technology.*[64]

B.   Information about available programmes:

The section 'Programmes in Print' from the *Yearbook of the Association for Programmed Learning and Educational Technology* is the most comprehensive source.[65]

The register of learning programmes compiled by the British Association for Commercial and Industrial Education is now out of date. The Programmed Instruction Centre for Industry (Sheffield University) provides literature mainly about programmes for operatives in industry.

There is a large number of unpublished learning programmes available. Some of these are listed in 'HELPIS' (*Higher Education Learning Programme Information Service*) published by the National Council for Educational Technology.[66]

In chemistry, a number of programmes are available from The Chemical Society, and also from the Programmed Learning Groups set up by the London University Institute of Education.[67] In both of these schemes, the emphasis is on obtaining cooperation in order to validate programmes on a wider scale than the authors can arrange. Thus, the programmes are provided on condition that validation data is forthcoming from the users.

The APLET yearbook is continually updated by contributions in 'Visual Education' and 'Programmed Learning and Educational Technology'.

The National Centre for Programmed Learning (Birmingham University) will provide information about centres. There is a National Network of Programmed Learning Centres with a secretary at Bradford Technical College.

A *Bibliography of Programmes and Presentation Devices* is annually published by Dr. Carl Hendershot, Delta College, University City, Michigan, U.S.A.

References

1. B. F. Skinner, *Harvard Educ. Rev.* **24**, 86 (1954); B. F. Skinner and J. G. Holland, *Teaching Machines and Programmed Learning* Vol. I, National Education Association of the United States, New York 1965.
2. D. E. Hoare, *Programmed Introduction to General and Physical Chemistry,* Wiley, London 1967.
3. J. B. Pattison, *A Programmed Introduction to Gas-Liquid Chromatography* Heyden & Son, London 1970.
4. J. D. Lassila, G. M. Barrow, M. E. Kenney, R. L. Little and W. E. Thompson, *Programmed Reviews of Chemical Principles,* Benjamin, New York 1970.

5. D. E. Billing, Proceedings of the British Universities Film Council Conference on Visual Media in Chemistry, University of Aston 1971.

6. J. L. Evans, L. E. Homme and R. Glaser, *J. Educ. Res.* **55**, 513 (1962).

7. D. E. Billing, learning programmes: (*a*) *Electronegativity* 1970; (*b*) *Electronic Screening and Effective Nuclear Charge* 1971; (*c*) *The Russell-Saunders Scheme for Spin-Orbit Coupling in Multi-Electron Atoms* 1971; (*d*) *Energy Levels in Transition Metal Complexes* 1970. (Unpublished).

8. *Science Foundation Course,* The Open University, Walton 1971.

9. E. Glynn, *Ethanol and Other Alcohols,* Nuffield Advanced Science, Penguin, London 1971.

10. D. R. Hogg, learning programmes: *Benzenediazonium Chloride, and the Reactions of Diazonium Salts* 1971. (Unpublished).

11. D. MacDuffie, *Inorganic Chemistry Programmes* 1971. (Unpublished).

12. D. E. Billing, tape/slide sequence: *Spectral and Magnetic Properties of Metal Complexes* 1971. (Unpublished).

13. D. E. Billing, audiotutorials: *Metal Complexes* 1972. (Unpublished).

14. G. O. M. Leith, *Second Thoughts on Programmed Learning* Occasional Paper No. 1, National Council for Educational Technology, London 1969.

15. *Programmed Learning, A Symposium,* National Centre for Programmed Learning, National Committee for Audio Visual Aids in Education, London 1966.

16. D. E. Billing, Proceedings of the Conference on Modern Science Teaching Methods, Liverpool Polytechnic 1972.

17. S. K. Gryde, *Audio Vis. Commun. Rev.* **14**, 71 (1966).

18. D. L. Moore, *Programmed Learning* **4**, 37 (1967); G. O. M. Leith and M. J. Tobin, *Visual Educ.,* 23 (1968).

19. N. A. Crowder, in *Automatic Teaching: The State of the Art,* E. Galanter (Ed.), Wiley, New York 1959.

20. S. M. Markle, *Good Frames and Bad,* Wiley, New York 1964.

21. E. Braun and E. T. Wait, *Programmed Problems in Thermodynamics,* McGraw-Hill, New York 1967.

22. B. N. Lewis and G. Pask, *Teaching Machines and Programmed Learning* Vol. 2, National Education Association of the United States, New York 1965, p. 213; G. Pask, in *Teaching Machines and Programming,* K. Austwick (Ed.), Pergamon, Oxford 1963.

23. L. Stolurow, in *Aspects of Educational Technology* Vol. 2, W. Dunn and C. Holroyd (Eds.), Methuen, London 1969; J. Annett and J. Duke (Eds.), *Proceedings of the Seminar on Computer Based Learning Systems, Leeds 1969,* National Council for Educational Technology, London 1970; L. M. Stolurow and D. Davis, *Teaching Machines and Programmed Learning* Vol. 2, National Education Association of the United States, New York 1965, p. 162.

24. K. Egan, *Programmed Learning and Educ. Technol.* 9, 63 (1972); A. M. Hodgson, *Chemical Structure,* University of London Press, London 1969.

25. M. R. Harris, structural communication: *Basic Physical Chemistry – Study Unit 14: Phase Diagrams* 1968. (Unpublished).

26. M. M. Orchin and H. H. Jaffé, *J. Chem. Educ.* **47**, 372 (1970).

27. T. F. Gilbert, *J. Mathetics.* **1**, 7 (1962).

28. R. M. Gagné, *Psychol. Rev.* **69**, 355 (1962); R. M. Gagné, *Teaching Machines and Programmed Learning* Vol. 2, National Education Association of the United States, New York 1965, p. 21.

29. H. Mathias, learning programme: *Interpretation of Infrared Spectra for Functional Groups* 1971. (Unpublished).

30. S. Pressey, *J. Psychol.* **29**, 417 (1950).

31. T. A. Whitworth, *School Sci. Rev.* **47**, 654 (1966); **48**, 721 (1967); K. Holling in *Media and Methods,* D. Unwin (Ed.), McGraw-Hill, London 1969.

32. G. O. M. Leith, *Handbook of Programmed Learning,* Educational Review Occasional Publications No. 1, University of Birmingham 1966.

33. M. Shayer, *Educ. Chem.* **7**, 182 (1970).
34. R. Glaser, in *Programmed Learning and Computer Based Instruction,* J. E. Coulson (Ed.), Wiley, New York 1962.
35. F. Mechner, *Programming for Automatic Instruction* Basic Systems Inc., N.Y. 1961; *Teaching Machines and Programmed Learning* Vol. 2, National Education Association of the United States, New York 1965, p. 441.
36. C. A. Thomas, I. K. Davies, D. Openshaw and J. B. Bird, *Programmed Learning in Perspective,* Lamson, London 1963.
37. A. J. Romiszowski, *Selection and Use of Teaching Aids,* Kogan Page, London 1968.
38. D. Rowntree, *Basically Branching,* MacDonald, London 1966.
39. P. Pipe, *Practical Programming,* Holt, Rinehart & Winston, London 1966.
40. C. S. Blake, in *Aspects of Educational Technology* Vol. 1, D. Unwin and J. Leedham (Eds.), Methuen, London 1966, p. 439.
41. H. Kay, B. Dodd and M. Sime, *Teaching Machines and Programmed Instruction,* Penguin, London 1968.
42. D. E. Hoare, personal communication 1971.
43. G. O. M. Leith, in *Media and Methods,* D. Unwin (Ed.), McGraw-Hill, London 1969.
44. C. Flood Page, *Technical Aids to Teaching in Higher Education,* Society for Research into Higher Education, London 1971.
45. J. Annett, in *New Horizons in Psychology,* B. M. Foss (Ed.), Penguin, London 1966.
46. W. Schramm, research on programmed learning: *Report on International Conference on Programmed Instruction and Teaching Machines,* Pädagogische Arbeitstelle, Berlin 1964, p. 462.
47. Schools Council Curriculum Bulletin No. 3 *Changes in School Science Teaching,* Evans/Methuen Education, London 1970.
48. R. M. Beard and D. Bligh, *Research into Teaching Methods in Higher Education,* Society for Research into Higher Education, London 1971.
49. R. M. Beard, *Teaching and Learning in Higher Education,* Penguin, London 1970.
50. J. Hartley, *Some Guides for Evaluating Programmes,* Association for Programmed Learning, London 1963.
51. S. J. Samuels, *Psychonomic Sci.* **16**, 67 (1969); W. J. McKeachie and W. Hiler, *J. Educ. Psychol.* **43**, 224 (1954).
52. J. Hartley and J. Holt, in *Aspects of Educational Technology* Vol. 4, A. C. Bajpai and J. F. Leedham (Eds.), Pitman, London 1970; J. Hartley, *Programmed Learning and Educ. Technol.* **9**, 108 (1972).
53. K. D. Duncan and T. Gilbert, *Brit. J. Educ. Psychol.* **36**, 4 (1966).
54. L. A. Biran and E. Pickering, *Brit. J. Med. Educ.* **2**, 213 (1968).
55. J. M. Newton and A. E. Hickey, *J. Educ. Psychol.* **54**, 140 (1965).
56. D. E. Hoare and M. Revans, *Aspects of Educational Technology* Vol. 2, W. Dunn and C. Holyroyd (Eds.), Methuen, London 1969, p. 303.
57. D. R. Hogg, in *Aspects of Educational Technology* Vol. 1, D. Unwin and J. Leedham (Eds.), Methuen, London 1966, p. 315; D. R. Hogg, *Educ. Chem.* **10**, 7 (1973).
58. G. O. M. Leith, in *Aspects of Educational Technology* Vol. 2, W. Dunn and C. Holyroyd (Eds.), Methuen, London 1969,, p. 107.
59. D. M. Brethower, *Programmed Instruction: A Manual of Programming Techniques,* Pitman, London 1963.
60. E. Stones, *Readings in Educational Psychology,* Methuen, London 1970.
61. K. Austwick (Ed.), *Teaching Machines and Programming,* Pergamon, Oxford 1964.
62. W. I. Smith and J. W. Moore, *Programmed Learning,* Van Nostrand, New York 1962.
63. R. Glaser (Ed.), *Teaching Machines and Programmed Learning* Vols. 1 & 2, National Education Association of the United States, New York 1965.

64. *Aspects of Educational Technology* Vols. 1-6, Association for Programmed
     Learning and Educational Technology, 1966-1972.
65. A. J. Romiszowski (Ed.), *Yearbook of the Association for Programmed Learning
     and Educational Technology,* Kogan Page, London 1972.
66. Higher Education Learning Programmes Information Service (HELPIS), No. 1,
     March 1971, National Council for Educational Technology, London.
67. R. M. Beard, *Chem. Brit.* 7, 324 (1971); M. D. Robinson, *Chem. Brit.* 7, 326
     (1971).

CHAPTER 12

Computer-based Learning in Laboratory Courses

P. B. AYSCOUGH

The computer based learning unit in the University of Leeds was set up in October 1969 following the award of an initial grant of £110,000 from the Science Research Council and the Social Sciences Research Council to the Department of Computational Science and the School of Education.

In the initial exploratory period seven main projects were undertaken ranging from primary school mathematics to university science, as follows:

1. *Primary School Mathematics* (in various local schools);
2. English as a second language (for immigrant children);
3. School Science (O-level Mechanics, A-level Physics);
4. University Mathematics for Applied Scientists;
5. *Applied Statistics* (Departments of Psychology and Education);
6. Clinical diagnosis (Department of Medicine, St. James' Hospital, Leeds);
7. *University Science* (Department of Physical Chemistry).

Projects (1), (5), (7) have been selected for the most intensive development after 1972.

The basic equipment in use consists of a Modular One computing system (16K sixteen bit word core store, 1M word disc, paper tape input and output, control teletype and communications multiplexer) together with eight remote teletypes and four audio-visual stations. The Modular One computer has been operating successfully with multi-access facilities since November 1970 using G.P.O. lines for connections outside the department. About 800 hours of teaching use of teletypes was achieved in the second term of the 1970-71 session and about 3,500 hours of teaching use are expected for 1971-72.

An author language of some generality and flexibility has been developed to facilitate the organization of teaching material for presentation at a terminal and, simultaneously, to assess student responses. The intention is that student responses should be as close to normal English as possible, with some facilities for use of mathematical and chemical formulae. An extended BASIC language for calculations will be available shortly.

The project involving the School of Chemistry is concerned with the teaching of practical Physical Chemistry to second year students. Our interest had arisen from our concern about the increasing dichotomy between lectures and laboratory work, and the lack of involvement of students in the design of the experiments they carry out. These problems are most common in large teaching departments where educationally desirable developments sometimes have to be sacrificed for administrative convenience. (In Leeds about 800 students take a course in practical Physical Chemistry each year: there are nearly 20 different courses varying in length from 4 to 22 weeks). It seemed to us that computer-based learning offered a unique solution to some of the problems involved by turning to advantage the major cause of the problems, namely the large size of the classes.

In order to examine the feasibility of using computer-based learning in the context of a laboratory course a number of teaching programmes were constructed with the following specific objectives:

1.   to ensure that the student has an adequate understanding of the theoretical background of the experiment which he proposes to carry out;

2.   to lead him to select the correct experimental procedure and to assist in planning the experimental details;

3.   to provide additional simulated data for experimental situations which are, for one reason or another, not accessible in the laboratory.

The programmes in use at the moment are concerned with experiments on solution equilibria and reaction kinetics. The three equilibria experiments are concerned with acid-base equilibria and the dissociation of complex ions. The experiments have a common theoretical background but involve a variety of experimental techniques including spectrophotometry, conductivity and pH measurements, the use of radio-active tracers and ion-exchange resins. Simulated data are provided for some studies of the effect of ionic strength on the dissociation of the complex ion $FeNCS^{2+}$. The experiments on reaction kinetics are also based on a common theoretical background and involve dilatometry, polarimetry and spectrophotometry.

Each programme requires 20-50 minutes to complete, depending on the student's skill and knowledge. The programmes take the form of questions set by the computer and responses made by the student via the teletype. Flexibility in computer response is obtained by means of a sophisticated system for matching the student response to the 'correct' answer. Matching is tight where mathematical relations are required but much looser where for instance definitions or explanations are asked for. Questions involving complicated equations, formulae or graphs can be presented by means of an automatic slide projector controlled by the computer. Data stored on file can be retrieved by the student when needed: teaching sub-routines are provided and can be brought into use when the student's responses show that he is in difficulties, or when the student asks for them. All questions and responses are printed out and the computer keeps a record of the student's performance based on the number of occasions help is sought and the kind of information requested. The programmes can be modified quite readily as and when necessary.In the first experiment, carried out in the Spring of 1971, a class of 32 students was divided into four groups of eight, one group acting as a control. The other three groups used different combinations of the available programmes and all then carried out the laboratory experiments in the normal manner. Students' reactions were then examined by questionnaire and by interview. Their experimental work and reports were marked independently by demonstrators in the usual manner.

A detailed report of the results of this and other experiments based on computer-based learning will be presented elsewhere but a few general observations may be of interest here. It is clear that, in general, students enjoyed the experience (though there is an obvious novelty value which will diminish with greater exposure). They learned the use of the teletype very rapidly and had no great difficulty in presenting their answers in a form acceptable to the computer. The difficulties which arose in this context were mainly the result of lack of clarity in the student's response, or insufficient precision in the phrasing of the question. All students felt that they had profited by being exposed to this persistent and anonymous questioner: most said that they preferred this to the alternative forms of pre-testing by multiple choice questions or by a demonstrator. Independent assessments of their experimental work showed a significantly better performance for those who had used both theory and planning programmes compared with the control group.

There is thus little doubt that an immediate benefit is derived from the enhanced awareness of the background theory and the factors involved in the design of the specific experiment being studied. However, some other studies which we hoped might show that knowledge of the design problems of one experiment would be reflected in improved performance in subsequent experiments were inconclusive possibly because the programmes being used were too specific.

In the current series of studies, involving about 90 students, attention is being concentrated on the planning programmes which are being constructed round a general planning algorithm which can be applied to a very wide range of laboratory experiments. We hope to learn the optimum balance between computer control and student control over the route taken through the programme and thus deal more efficiently with a wider range of abilities in the users.

An essential feature of the kind of computer-based learning being investigated in Leeds is its interactive nature and its capability for individualized instruction. This is the feature which places computer-based learning in a quite different category from programmed learning and may ultimately make it more acceptable as a teaching method. Several large-scale projects in American universities, concerned with general instruction in Chemistry and in problem-solving, are producing encouraging results. We believe that our application of computer-based learning to laboratory work is unique: we hope that it may be especially beneficial in adding a new dimension to the role of the teaching laboratory.

CHAPTER 13

Production of Chemistry Television Programmes

A. R. TATCHELL

This paper is based on the author's experience over the past few years, of writing, presenting and helping to produce television programmes on chemistry for the educational television (E.T.V.) network of the Inner London Education Authority (I.L.E.A.). The purpose is to briefly outline the scope and the mechanism for the production of programmes in this area, and to discuss the kind of problems which can arise.

Chemistry programmes for transmission on the I.L.E.A.-E.T.V. network have been produced for courses appropriate to the Further Education and Higher Education fields. In the former case, ideas are submitted to an I.L.E.A.-Advisory Panel and its appointed working parties, for approval and correlation with programme ideas in other subject areas. Such ideas originate from the staff of the F.E. and H.E. establishments within the London area, and programme production takes place in the I.L.E.A.-E.T.V. studios.

In the Higher Education field, programme ideas are selected by subject working parties, set up under the guidance of the Liaison Officer (Mr. N. Collins), having representatives of the Colleges of the University of London, the City University and the five London Polytechnics. Programmes are produced in the studios of the Audio-Visual Centre of the University of London, the City University and the City of London Polytechnic.

Programmes for both the F.E. and H.E. channels are transmitted by Post Office Line to all educational establishments within the London area. Details of programme times and copies of booklets, which supply background information and which re-iterate and expand technical points and practical points discussed in the relevant programmes, may be obtained from the I.L.E.A.-E.T.V. Centre.

At the present time (December 1971) the following programme series, appropriate to chemistry and allied subjects, have been produced and transmitted on these two channels; other titles are of course projected:

1. The Chemical Industry;

2. Introduction to Plastics;
3. Material Science;
4. Instrumental Methods of Analysis;
5. Handling Radioisotopes in the Laboratory;
6. Techniques in Organic Chemistry.

The educational aims in each of these programme series have naturally not been identical. In general, they have been designed to fulfill one or more of the following functions for A-level, H.N.C. or first year University courses—

(*a*) to provide an introductory treatment of selected theoretical topics followed by an expanded development in greater depth to stimulate further thought and discussion;

(*b*) to consider the application of experimental techniques that would not otherwise be possible in an experimental course, as well as a detailed and practical view of essential laboratory techniques;

(*c*) to provide supplementary illustrative material drawn from industrial situations, and to view equipment which may not be available at individual Colleges.

Programme series fulfilling other functions are being considered by the appropriate working parties, and it is hoped within a few years to have a comprehensive library of recorded programmes to meet a range of educational needs.

The members of staff of the F.E. and H.E. establishments who suggest programme ideas are usually responsible for writing the detailed scripts. In the case of programmes for the F.E. Channel, a Director of a programme series is appointed from a group of I.L.E.A. teachers seconded to the E.T.V. service. These teachers are selected on the basis of their performance in a multi-stage television training programme, and they provide, by their participation in the E.T.V. services as Directors and Presenters for Primary, Secondary and Further Educational programmes, the essential link between the television studios and the class or lecture room. There is a close liaison between the appointed Director of a Programme Series (together with the professional and technical staff of the E.T.V. Centre) and the script writers concerned with the translation of a programme idea into the finished video-tape recording.

Since the general problems which arise in production could be common to most scientific and technological programmes, it is perhaps pertinent to review some of the difficulties which have been encountered in the production of series 3, 4 and 6 and suggest means by which they may be avoided.

SCRIPT WRITING

In short programmes (about 10 min.) which aim to demonstrate or expound on a *single* operation—whether this be an experimental technique or a theoretical concept—and where the number of cameras and camera movements is limited, there are arguments against a scripted programme. One of the strongest is that spontaneity is severely restricted. On the other hand, for longer and more complex programmes, in which several themes are developed and several cameras and many camera movements are involved, the use of a script is essential if a high standard is to be maintained. However, within such a script there is usually ample opportunity for *ad lib* comments and sequences which, if skilfully interposed, can give the script a fluency which would otherwise be missing.

The script must be written in the spoken word and if possible in the natural idiom of the presenter. An obvious point is that there should be economy of words and clarity of meaning; too much verbiage is wasteful of time and confusing to the listeners. At the other extreme, short breathless statement must also be avoided. The script should always be checked and double-checked by the other script writers and the presenter concerned in the programme series to avoid ambiguities.

The author will also need to indicate on his script what sequence of captions, models and demonstrations are required. Whilst the final decision as to the best method of presentation of these items will rest with the Director, nevertheless the author should have clearly in mind not only what will be achieved by such aids to his script, but also be aware of the limitations of camera movements. In this connection, it is helpful if script-writers have taken advantage of a television training course such as those which the I.L.E.A. organizes from time to time.

PRESENTER

There is in most lecturers, who have the inclination to become involved in educational television, an extrovert element which enables them to project the subject matter in an interesting and lively manner. Nevertheless, insufficient familiarity with the medium, coupled with the knowledge that the sequence of movements and operations of the camera crew and the production team rests entirely on the presenter keeping to the agreed sequence (whether scripted or supposedly *ad lib*), tends to daunt the new-comer, so that the projected image may be stilted, inadequate and disappointing to all concerned. Furthermore, the viewer will almost certainly compare, unconsciously, the presentation with the standard of B.B.C. and I.T.V. documentary programmes. In the Programme Series 3 and 4, most of the individual programmes used an auto-cue* (*see* interview below) and this at least relieved the presenter of remembering the scripted sections. However, even the use of an auto-cue generates problems, not the least of which is that the script sounds as though it is being read and the pace of presentation is too fast. Thus familiarity with the script by the presenter is essential, so that he may be seen to be thinking about the subject matter. The relative emphasis on words, the pace of talking and the interest of the topic then fall into perspective and this provides a way out of the difficulty. A relaxed presentation is also encouraged, not so much by looking at the camera lenses, as by a mental projection to the invisible group beyond the lenses.

CAPTIONS

A good caption, like a good slide must not carry too much information. Frequently it is profitable to build up the final caption by a series of 'reveals' timed to coincide with

* An auto-cue is an illuminated screen attached to the front of the camera. The script is projected onto the screen, and the presenter can thus read the script whilst apparently looking directly at the camera.

the scripted word. Both the still and animated captions require careful checking, to avoid 'artists impressions' of graphs or apparatus leading to an incorrect representation. It cannot be too strongly emphasized that an animated caption can frequently make a point more clearly than the spoken word. The advice of the 'Graphics Department' is invaluable in this connection.

MODELS

There is an inherent difficulty with the use of molecular and crystal models in that a three dimensional concept is being projected onto a two dimensional screen. This, coupled with the fact that only black, white and varying shades of grey distinguish the various parts of the three dimensional model, results in a fairly unsatisfactory screen image. One way of improving the situation is to show the models being handled by the presenter, since the various stereochemical features may then be easily pointed out. Some success was achieved in this direction by showing an addition-polymerization process using models. It has also been found that the facilities of superimposition provided by two cameras greatly aid the explanation of, for example, hybridization of atomic orbitals.

APPARATUS AND DEMONSTRATIONS

Perhaps two of the most valuable uses of the television techniques arise, firstly from the possibility of showing, to a large group of students, pieces of apparatus which they may not have had the opportunity of seeing before; and secondly, of showing them in clear detail parts of the apparatus, and its operation, that cannot be viewed simultaneously by each individual in the live situation.

Examples of the former case are analytical and preparative gas chromatographic equipment, ultraviolet and infrared spectrophotometers, nuclear magnetic resonance and mass spectrometers and atomic emission spectrophotometers. Examples of the latter case are a camera close-up of the melting process, in which the bottom of a melting-point tube occupies a significant proportion of the screen; a close-up of the dropping mercury electrode and a glass electrode, the filling and positioning of ultraviolet or infrared cells, and the loading of gas chromatographic columns.

Demonstrations of equipment are also valuable, but the results need to be very critically examined for errors of technique. These arise particularly after several rehearsals in which various camera angles and positions have been examined, when even a very familiar sequence of technical operations may become subject to serious omissions. Nevertheless, informative demonstrations of the operation of spectrometers, pH meters, polarographs etc., have been successfully completed.

INTERVIEWS

In the limited experience of the author, an interview situation provides the best opportunity for an informal and relaxed presentation of material. Clearly it would no be applicable to all programme material, but it should be used wherever possible. Such a programme could not be conveniently produced using an auto-cue for the participants. This means that the detailed phraseology of the discussion is largely improvised around a series of area headings. In this sort of situation, it is of course essential that the interview (presenter) carefully leads the discussion by the introduction of the various themes and their subsequent development. The fact that both participants are talking to each other rather than to an inanimate lens, would appear to be the major reason why the results are more satisfactory with newcomers to the medium.

SUMMARY

The television medium is being increasingly used, along with other visual aids, as a means of providing an extension to the formal lecture or informal tutorial situation. Some of the dangers inherent in this development have been referred to in another paper,[1] and the full benefits of the medium will only be achieved by a detailed formulation of objectives, an insistence on high programme standards, and by careful attention to the needs and attitudes of the students. As more programme series become linked with specific courses, so the availability of the video-tapes and facilities offered to students for private study will have to be examined.

Acknowledgements

The help, advice and expertise freely given by the permanent and seconded members of staff of the E.T.V. Centre has been greatly appreciated and in particular thanks are due to Arthur Phillips and David Stewart who were the Directors of Programme Series 3 and 4 respectively.

Reference

1. L. R. B. Elton, in *Aims, Methods and Assessment in Advanced Science Education,* D. E. Billing and B. S. Furniss (Eds.), Heyden & Son, London 1973, p. 69 (this volume).

IV. ASSESSMENT METHODS

CHAPTER 14

Forms of Assessment in Tertiary Education

R. COX

Consider the following imaginary reference:

1. John Brown works hard at courses which interest him, but not otherwise. His coverage is, therefore, very patchy—this is the main reason for the three particularly low combined marks.

2. Within courses his factual knowledge is below average but his knowledge of arguments and principles is good. His application of theory to new situations is often ingenious, but he shows little awareness of limitations. At a theoretical level he shows high ability in analysis, but in empirical situations he tends to get lost if he must deal with a large amount of factual data.

3. He will readily attempt to synthesize ideas from diverse fields and such attempts are often very suggestive. His enthusiasm, however, appears to prevent a healthy critical approach to his own work. In evaluating the work of others, he is more open-minded and can extract what is important from work which is opposed to his own ideas.

4. Generally, he works better in open situations, but his concise logical style enables him to adapt to constraints of time and space, without serious distortions.

5. With empirical projects his statistical work is competent, but lacks flexibility and sensitivity in dealing with complex data. With theoretical projects he shows great enthusiasm and his work is consistently of a high standard.

6. In seminars, he expresses ideas clearly and with conviction, but is not a good listener and quickly shows impatience.

We might suspect that such a reference could be very subjective, and because at present the system does not encourage lecturers to spend much time on such complex assessments, it may well be inaccurate. Instead we concentrate an enormous amount of effort on the official method, which gives a result like '2(i)'. It is very difficult to make sense of this particular situation, but it is often argued that the degree classification sums everything up because all the students' abilities are positively associated.

RELATIONSHIPS BETWEEN ABILITIES

Students, however, often concentrate on topics in which they do not have high abilities, in order to compensate at the assessment stage. Thus, they can adapt to the system and the correlations between abilities which appear, may obscure genuine differences. Table 14.1, however, shows correlation coefficients (r), calculated by Tyler (Zoology)[1] and by McGuire, (Medicine),[2] between attainments of different objectives where special efforts were made to test them separately and reliably. They are all low, suggesting that there is little association of the abilities.

Table 14.1. Intercorrelations between Attainments in Different Objectives

R. W. Tyler[1] *Zoology*	r
Understanding Technical Terms/Ability to Draw Inferences from facts	·35
Information/Ability to apply Principles to concrete situations	·40
Information/Ability to formulate experiments to test hypotheses	·46
Memory/Skill in the use of microscope	·02
C. McGuire[2] *(Medicine)*	r (range)
Problem Solving/Recall of Information	·18—·41
Ability to Interpret Data/Conventional Exam	·08—·25

At the University of Essex, we tried to diversify the assessment system in sociology. We found virtually no correlations for any given subject, between traditional examinations, open (5 weeks to complete) examinations and course-work essays. However, if the comparisons were calculated not on the basis of each subject, but on the basis of the two best marks for each subject (irrespective of subject), we did find a definite relationship between examinations and course-work. This suggests that intercorrelations between different forms of assessment are dependent upon students' relative ability or involvement in relation to particular subjects.

Black,[3] McGuire[2] and Drever,[4] have all investigated the types of ability being measured by traditional examinations. Black analysed a large number of physics examination questions, finding that about 40 per cent depended almost entirely on memory. Drever also found that whatever first year Physics and Psychology papers assessed, it was soon forgotten after the examination. This was shown by the failure of 120 first year students (out of about 300) when unexpectedly given the same examination they had passed six weeks earlier.

There is a great need now, not for graduates with excellent memories of factual data, but for those with more varied skills and flexibility. Reflecting on ability dimension in human society, Faris[5] says 'we might have to revise our notions of what goes into human ability and its manifestations for performance. Where society becomes increasingly complex and at the same time dynamic, the problem of defining the ability required in each new situation may turn out to be practically insoluble.' The need for flexibility, is stressed by Leach,[6] by Swann[7] and by Schon[8] who links it with the question of personal identity: 'If we are losing stable values and anchors for personal identity how can we maintain a sense of self-respect and self-identity while in the very process of change?'

STUDENTS' VIEWS ON ASSESSMENT

When questioned, some students say that they came to university for vocational reasons, but the problem of identity, seems to be increasingly important. More students are now wondering why they come to university. This may lead to high 'wastage rates'—Wanowski[9] has shown that 'wastage' is related to a lack of clear goals and a lack of involvement in the decision to enter higher education. Student's views of course objectives are often influenced by their perception of the demands imposed on them by the system of assessment, but this can be very discouraging from an educational point of view.

Stallings & Leslie[10] investigated student attitudes towards grading at the University of Illinois. Their results are given in Table 14.2. There was remarkable unanimity amongst various faculties. Whether or not the students' picture of the grading is accurate, it is important to remember that evidence shows that perception of a situation can seriously affect responses to it.

Table 14.2. Student Attitudes towards Grades and Grading. (A = Agree or strongly agree, D = Disagree or strongly disagree). (From Stallings and Leslie[10])

	A%	D%
Encourage cheating	80	18
Restrict Study to Test Material	91	7
Despite instructors' insistence that they do not teach 'facts' most grades are based on tests which are primarily factual in content	84	14
Emphasis placed on grades encourages students to conform on tests and in the class-room to the instructors' views and opinions	85	12
Grading system tends to reward the conforming student and penalize the imaginative student	60	37
Grades provide me with the motive to do assigned course work	65	32
Grades provide 'feed-back' telling me if I have learned the material	37	60

The following comments on assessment from sociology students at Essex University may be rather stronger than most students but they illustrate themes which are common and significant:

1. 'Writing four questions in a three-hour exam is a total contradiction of what you have been training yourself to do throughout the year.'

2. 'The more cold-blooded you can become, the better—you have got to make yourself like a machine. The exam is the compulsory part of being a student, the essay is part of your role of being an individual. You put yourself into it, you are personally much more involved in it.'

3. 'If I were really worried about getting a 2(i) I'd be dead scared of the people here. I'd be rushing around to do things which people do to impress. I've written it off

because I don't think—without distorting my personality beyond recognition—I could
get a 2(i) in this place—I would have to conform to the right model.'

4.   'I don't look upon myself as a good examinee . . . I am so stupid and weak
minded, I just go on and on completely oblivious to time . . . no not oblivious, worried
about it, but having some compulsion to write.'

For a scientist, the project might achieve the importance which the second student
saw in the essay. The eventual success of these students (all obtained a 1st or 2(i)
degree class), shows that some students can adapt to what they see is a bad system and
that not all criticism is 'sour grapes'. Other sources of students' criticism of examinations are the N.U.S. pamphlets.[12]

DIVERSIFICATION OF ASSESSMENTS

I can only give a brief outline of some of the ways in which systems are being diversified to cover a wider range of different course objectives.

Open Examinations

The English Department at the University of York has experimented with sessional
examinations in which students take the paper away and have fourteen days to write
answers. This differs from course-work, in that there is a space limit (2,000 words)
imposed upon the essays which requires students to be very careful of their priorities
and pay more attention to organization. Coming at the end of the year this assessment
encourages students to synthesize their ideas more than ordinary essays.

Prior Notice Examination

In this case, the paper is given out say fourteen days before the examination, but a day
is appointed on which the students come to an examination room to answer the paper.
This may seem to emphasize memory, but this is only true if the questions stress recall
abilities. Students react differently to relaxation of time and memory constraints;
most in sociology found it liberating but about 25 per cent get over-involved in hectic
reading before the examination, as a response to the higher expectations.

Open Book Examination

Engineering students at Bradford, Liverpool and Southampton responded well to final
examinations into which they were allowed to take books. Page (Chemical Engineering)[13] thought that such examinations lead to an 'understanding and appreciation of
the limitations of existing knowledge of engineering science', that they lead to an
awareness of other disciplines, and that much care was needed in their design. 'We
believe that it has a profound effect on the type of question, on teaching method, and
on students' consciousness and approach to learning. Much less time is spent on
memory work than hitherto.'

Oral Examinations

Although oral examinations tend to be unreliable,[14] they could be tightened up by specifying objectives, the attainment of which we are trying to measure. In this case, they could play an important part in a more diversified and open assessment system. The main use of such methods at present is to check on problems arising from other forms of assessment. However, they could be used to assess communication skills, which are very important to scientists who work in teams and who also have a responsibility of explaining their work more widely. At York, the assessment of oral contributions to seminars was successful and not too inhibiting.[13] In this form a continuous assessment, rather than a final oral examination, is used.

Projects

These are being used increasingly now for both individuals and groups, and seem to be very effective for motivation.

No correlation was found between engineering examinations and project marks.[15] Whiteland[16] found that half of the best writers of geography projects did not get class 1 or 2(i) degrees. Generally, the small amount of research on such relationships shows low correlations. Projects therefore appear to assess different abilities to other methods of assessment, yet they are perhaps the most relevant form of assessment for the graduate who will proceed to research work, and have an important role in motivation.[17]

Objective Tests

These are dealt with in another paper. Their essential contribution to assessment is to measure quickly the achievement of a large number of objectives relating to knowledge, comprehension and rather simple applications. This complements the other methods of assessment, which can then concentrate on higher-level abilities.

Self-assessment

Self-assessment methods have been used in conjunction with project work, particularly in architecture and town planning. Students may judge each other's projects in a group assessment, but the results of such grading need not be included in the final mark. L. Thomas at Brunel University is currently working in this field and finds that it is useful for staff to contribute to discussions by emphasizing criteria of judgement with students concentrating on particular pieces of work. Role-playing and simulation methods often involve student self-assessment.

CONCLUSIONS

As we begin to use a wider variety of assessment methods, so more emphasis is likely to be put on more open forms both inside and outside the examination room. Trust then becomes more important and the student may exploit the greater freedom in two ways by—

(*a*)   abusing it through plagiarism or dull conformity, to obtain higher marks; or more constructively;

(*b*)   by using the opportunities to explore and develop his own abilities and interests.

The whole ethos of the institution, as well as the work load on the student, may affect the choice of abuse or use. If the course structure is not changed to match the new methods, it may well become too demanding and the student may adopt educationally dubious strategies to cope with it. But if a more open and varied system of assessment can be made to work, then the link between adolescent drives for identity and autonomy on the one hand, and academic work on the other may be strengthened in particularly constructive ways.

References

1. R. W. Tyler, in *The Learning Process,* T. Harris and W. Schwahn (Eds.), Oxford University Press, New York 1961.
2. C. McGuire, in *Conference on Medical Education in South Africa,* J. Reid and A. Wilmot (Eds.), Natal University Press 1964.
3. P. J. Black, *Phys. Educ.* 3, 93 (1968).
4. J. Drever, *On Examinations,* Talk given to National Association of Schoolmasters, April 1965, unpublished.
5. R. Faris, *Amer. Sociol. Rev.* 26, 835 (1961).
6. E. Leach, The Rieth Lectures 1967 (especially 'Man and Learning'), *The Listener* 14 December 1967.
7. 'The Flow into Employment of Scientists, Engineers and Technologists' (Swann Report), H.M.S.O., London 1971.
8. D. Schon, *Beyond the Stable State,* Temple Smith, London 1971.
9. J. Wankowski, *Some Aspects of Motivation in Success and Failure at University,* 4th Annual Conference, Society for Research into Higher Education, London 1968.
10. W. M. Stallings and K. Leslie, *Improving College and University Teaching* Vol. XVIII No. 1, 1970, p. 66.
11. R. Rosenthal and L. Jacobsen, *Sci. Amer.* 218, 19 (1968).
12. National Union of Students, *N.U.S. Executive Report on Examinations,* National Union of Students, London 1969.
13. *Assessment of Undergraduate Performance,* Committee of Vice Chancellors and Principals, and Association of University Teachers, London 1969.
14. R. Cox, *Univ. Quart.* 21.3, 292-340 (1967).
15. P. Allen, in *Innovations and Experiments in University Teaching Methods,* Conference Report, University Teaching Methods Unit, London Institute of Education 1968.
16. J. W. Whiteland, *Univ. Quart.* 21.1, 4 (1966).
17. P. J. Black, N. A. Dyson and D. O'Connor, *Phy. Educ.* 3, 289 (1968).

CHAPTER 15

An Analysis of University Chemistry Examinations

A. W. MACKAILL

In trying to assess chemical ability, teachers at all levels are faced with two very closely related problems:
1. What constitutes chemical ability?
2. Do examinations in Chemistry measure chemical ability and if so, do they measure it consistently?

The descriptions of various types of abilities, in terms of the achievement of objectives, have been considered in earlier chapters; this contribution therefore deals with problem (2)—in other words are chemistry examinations valid and are they reliable?

THE ASSESSMENT OF OBJECTIVES

An attempt has already been made[1] to define the objectives of chemistry teaching, in terms of 'recall', 'application' and 'Scientific Method'. For the purpose of studying the extent to which they have been examined, the objectives have been grouped as involving:

A. Recall ability;
B. More complex abilities (application, scientific method).

For the year 1969, chemistry lecturers at Heriot-Watt University, Edinburgh, were asked to prepare examination marking schemes to indicate percentages of (A) and (B) abilities being examined in each of their questions.

Table 15.1 shows the results for the 1969 Organic Chemistry paper. Indices of facility* (F) and popularity (P) are listed, besides percentages of type A and type B abilities. This shows that questions 1-4 almost entirely recall abilities, while questions

---

* Facility Index = Mean score obtained by those students who answered the question, expressed as a percentage of the possible marks for the question.

Table 15.1. Analysis of Organic Chemistry Paper for 1969 Showing Facility Value (F),
Popularity (P) and Objectives Tested (A) and (B) for Each Question

Question	F	P	A	B
1	64	43	90	10
2	100	3	90	10
3	68	85	90	10
4	72	80	90	10
5	68	89	50	50
6	64	14	0	100
7	56	34	0	100
8	64	31	50	50
	mean:		58	42

5 and 6 are entirely different. The rank order correlation coefficient† between facility and popularity was $\rho = 0.12$ which is not significantly different from zero. Choice is therefore unrelated to marks scored.

Allowing for the variations of objectives tested by each question and the choice of questions allowed to the examiners, it seemed quite possible that individual students were being tested on the basis of substantially different objectives.

We investigated this possibility, and Table 15.2 shows the results for the two extreme groups (in terms of percentages of recall). Eight students have been examined on the basis of 80 per cent recall, and one on the basis of 25 per cent recall. The students' freedom of choice therefore results in an examination which is not the same for all students. This inequality is compounded by students' inability to select the easiest questions.

Table 15.2. Objectives Tested for Individual Students—Organic Chemistry 1969

	No. of students	A	B
High A	8	80	20
Low A	1	25	75
Mean for Class	35	52	38

The exercise was repeated for the 1969 Inorganic and Physical Chemistry papers. Two questions on the inorganic paper were almost entirely testing recall, while one was almost entirely testing higher abilities. The average taken over all eight questions was 64 per cent A and 36 per cent B. The rank order correlation between F and P was again very close to zero ($\rho = -0.11$). Three students were examined on the basis of 76 per cent recall while another answered questions requiring 49 per cent recall. The average for the class was 70 per cent A and 30 per cent B.

† p expresses the degree to which the order of questions ranked according to popularity corresponds with the order when questions are ranked in order of facility. It lies between −1 (perfect inverse relationship) to +1 (perfect direct relationship).

The analysis of the physical chemistry paper revealed a good correlation between choice of question and marks scored. The percentages of types of ability varied, but not quite so extremely as in the other two papers. The mean for each question was 44 per cent A + 56 per cent B. However, estimates of objectives tested for individual students did vary widely. Ten students were examined on the basis of 58 per cent recall while one student was examined on 35 per cent recall material, and the average was 51 per cent.

DISCRIMINATING POWER OF QUESTIONS

A qualitative estimate of the more popular questions was made in the following way. The candidates who answered the questions were ranked in order of their scores for the complete paper. The rank order was divided into sixths and the mean mark for the question calculated for each sixth. This was plotted on a histogram, the shape of the histogram giving a qualitative estimate of the discriminating power of the question. This analysis was carried out for the three most popular questions in each paper. Typical results are shown in Fig. 15.1 (1968 Physical Chemistry).

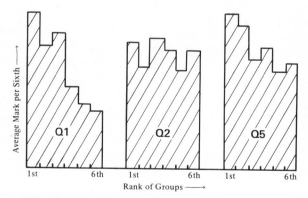

Fig. 15.1 Discrimination (Physical Chemistry 1968)

In this paper Q1 discriminates well, Q5 reasonably and Q2 not at all. It is interesting to note that, on the basis of these questions, the best discriminators are those questions with the lowest proportion of recall material. It was not possible to make a useful analysis of the less popular questions as in most cases too few students attempted them. Similar results were obtained for the other 1968 and 1969 papers.

This study of the discriminating power of a question suffers from two weaknesses. Firstly, the number of students selecting the questions is small even with the most popular questions; it varies from twenty-four to thirty, depending on the question. Consequently, the mean mark scored by one sixth of the rank order is based, in some cases, on only four or five students. Secondly, the choice of questions afforded to each student is four from eight. It follows that the score obtained by a candidate on any particular question is a relatively high proportion of his score on the paper as a whole.

The shape of the histogram may possibly be determined to some extent by the candidate's rank order on the question itself, The criteria on which the sixths are based, namely the candidates' total score, is open to doubt because of variable choices. The method gives a rough indication that examination questions do not discriminate identically.

CONCLUSIONS

The foregoing results show that the questions considered were not of equal difficulty, did not test objectives equally and did not discriminate equally.

The factors which operate when a student makes a choice of four questions from eight are not easy to identify. As already pointed out, it may be that certain questions are more attractive to better students. Clearly further research is required into how choices of questions are made.

It is important to make certain that all questions, as far as possible—

(*a*)   test objectives equally;
(*b*)   are equally difficult;
(*c*)   discriminate equally.

In the absence of such assurances, the use of wide choices, such as four questions attempted from a choice of eight set, should be avoided. This conclusion is particularly important when consideration is given to the range of material presented in tertiary level courses in chemistry. The traditions of wide choice were a recognition of the load undergone by candidates. If this heavy load is to be maintained, our studies imply the need for much greater attention to the nature of the objectives which examinations set out to measure. There appear to be a number of ways by which these ends can be achieved:

1.   A choice can be afforded if the question paper is divided into several sections, each section containing questions which are identical in the objectives which they measure. The students would then be allowed to choose say, two questions from each section. In this way there would be no variation from student to student in the objectives examined. To the best of our knowledge this suggestion for the sectioning of University examination papers on the basis of objectives has not previously been proposed.

2.   Each question in the paper could be an internal choice of the 'Either A or B' variety. Questions 5A and 5B (say) would be objectively identical, students attempting either A or B, and all questions in the paper would be compulsory.

3.   While methods (1) and (2) ensure that the same objectives are examined for all students, they do not ensure both content and objectives are properly sampled. It is possible to avoid this fault by constructing a matrix, the axes of which contain the content of the course (or part thereof) and the list of objectives. In a conventional examination, a matrix could be drawn up for each question and positive decisions about the number of marks to be awarded for a question (or part of a question) dealing with (say) the reactions of compound X at the application level, the number of marks being recorded in the appropriate 'cell'. Using this method, an examination may be constructed which adheres accurately to departmental policy on what requires to be tested and at which intellectual level.

It has been shown by Daterline[2] that students spend a great deal of time trying to discover what the objectives of a teaching course are. In other words, chemistry students are trying to discover how the chemistry staff define chemical ability. It is then clear, from various analyses of examination papers[1,3,4] that an ability to recall information is thought to be of some importance. The belief held by the majority of students is that the more complex abilities are unimportant when the aim is to *pass* a chemistry examination. Quite clearly the objectives of the course should be clearly delineated before any lectures on content are given.

It is necessary, then, to remind students of the existence of more complex intellectual skills and to point out that these are just as examinable as recall. If students assume that the recall of factual information is the *sine qua non* of University chemical education, they will of necessity fail to appreciate the more complex objectives and wider aims of that education, which must result in the production of a poorer chemist.

References

1. B. G. Gowenlock, D. M. McIntosh and A. W. Mackaill, *Chem. Brit.* **6**, 341 (1970).
2. W. A. Daterline, *Educ. Technol.* **8**, 7 (1968).
3. R. W. Crossland and R. Amos, *Biol. and Hum. Affairs* **26**, 38 (1961).
4. R. W. Crossland and R. Amos, *Biol. and Hum. Affairs* **30**, 35 (1965).

CHAPTER 16

Objective Tests in Tertiary Science Courses

D. E. BILLING

The aims of this paper are to answer the following questions:
1.   What are objective tests?
2.   How are they related to other methods of assessment?
3.   What can they assess?
4.   What are fixed-response items, and what are the main types of items?
5.   What examples of each of these items may be drawn from the area of tertiary science?
6.   What are the advantages and disadvantages of each type of item, and of objective testing as a whole?
7.   In what ways may such tests be used?
8.   What procedure should be followed in order to construct items, to assemble them into a test, to carry out the test, and to analyse the results of the test?
9.   What are the common faults in each type of item, and how may they be eliminated?

THE NATURE OF OBJECTIVE TESTS

It is important to distinguish two interrelated meanings:
   (*a*)   A method of testing for the attainment of specified objectives,
   (*b*)   A testing method which excludes the influence of subjective factors (e.g. emotions, disagreement over interpretation of questions, disagreement over the sophistication required of answers) so as to produce reliable results.

In this connection, *reliability* means that an individual candidate's score will not significantly vary if he takes the test again, or if he is marked by a different examiner. The first meaning stresses, instead, the *validity* of the test, that is its ability to measure the attainment of the objective which was specified. It may be useful to compare validity with reliability in the same way as accuracy and precision are compared in the measurement of physical quantities. Fig. 16.1 illustrates this point.

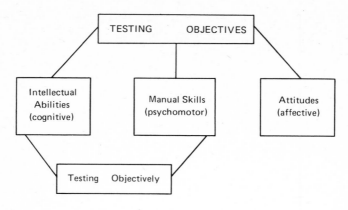

Fig. 16.1

TESTING OBJECTIVES

We may choose to test for abilities, aptitudes, attitudes, interests, motivation, personality traits etc. Those abilities associated with the manipulation and understanding of knowledge may be further classified. Some of these classifications of objectives have been discussed in Chap. 3. The relationship between objectives and assessment items is clear in the construction of learning programmes. Thus, an objective is converted directly into an assessment item, which appears in the post-test (and pre-test) and as a terminal frame in a learning sequence within the programme. Preceding frames build up the ability to negotiate each terminal frame (*see* Chap. 11).

TESTING OBJECTIVELY[1,2,3]

This is the meaning which is most commonly linked with objective testing. It is best seen as a subdivision of the testing of objectives, since it has always been stressed that objectives should be specified before test items are constructed. Hence, the considerations of the previous section are still relevant here—we attempt to test objectives objectively. This inevitability excludes certain types of aims, such as the assessment of attitudes or personality factors. There are no uniquely correct answers to questions on these areas, nor are the tests reliable if the aim is simply a description of an individual person. His answers may be dependent on the circumstances of the questions, and may not truly reveal his feelings. Tests must be very subtly constructed if the object of the test is not to be revealed.

In objective tests, on the other hand, we make clear the objectives being assessed. In the Open University courses, the students are given lists of overall course aims and of the objectives of each course unit. Self-Assessment items are in fact keyed to the relevant objectives, computer-marked assignments are based on unit objectives and (in the Science Foundation Course), the examination is based only on the overall course aims.[4]

An example of Self-Assessment Questions is given below:

Objective: Use electron repulsion theory to deduce the approximate shape of a simple covalent molecule.

Test: The bond angle in carbon dioxide CO_2 is expected to be:
   (i) $90°$
   (ii) $120°$
   (iii) $180°$
   (iv) None of the above

The following question is taken from the Open University Specimen Science Examination.

Course objective 9: demonstrate an understanding of some of the relations between technology and society.

Question: You are given a list of 10 scientific facts. Use your knowledge of the course (units 10, 13) and, where relevant, the supplementary information to assess the consequences of the discovery of the facts, by indicating in each case whether the direct application of the discovery has to date:

A.   had no social consequence;
B.   given rise to other developments which are socially advantageous but which in addition have created new problems for society;
C.   given rise to socially advantageous developments, apparently free from any direct major draw-backs or disadvantages.

Also indicate your confidence, which will be taken into account:
   (*a*)   completely confident
   (*b*)   very confident
   (*c*)   moderately confident
   (*d*)   slightly confident

(Supplementary information: ....)

   1.   A crystal of quartz is just one giant molecule.
   2.   Organic molecules are broken down and synthesized in living organisms with the aid of certain protein molecules (enzymes).
   3.   Methane, CH_4, combines with oxygen in a reaction which liberates a considerable amount of heat.
   4.   The organic compounds responsible for the physiological effects of many animal and plant materials on man, have been isolated and their chemical structures determined.
   5.   Polyvinylchloride (PVC) loses its rigidity and becomes pliable when mixed with small quantities of low molecular weight esters.
   6.   There is more than one possible structure for any hydrocarbon molecule with more than three carbon atoms.
   7.   DDT, an organochlorine compound, is highly toxic to insects but leaves plants unaffected.
   8.   The introduction of a polar or a hydrogen-bonding group into a coloured organic molecule enables it to adhere firmly to a surface composed of other polar or hydrogen-bodning groups.
   9.   Detergents with straight chain hydrocarbon fragments are much more easily broken down by micro-organisms than are those with branched chains.
   10.   The shape of methane, CH_4, is that of a tetrahedron with carbon at its centre and the four hydrogen atoms at the corners.

There are two main types of test item which have unambiguous answers:

(a)   **Constructed-response items,** sometimes called short-answer questions. Here the item is constructed so that the answer is a single word, number sign or phrase; the student writes this down. Some examples of short-answer questions are given below:

1. State the shape of each of the following molecules:
   (i) $COCl_2$
   (ii) SF_6
   (iii) SO_2
2. In what region of the spectrum of H is the Lyman series found?

A variant of the short-answer question is the linear learning programme (*see* Chap. 11). In the normal use of a programme for learning, the answers to each question are supplied. However, if the answers are omitted, the result is an extended series of constructed response questions. This may have the disadvantage that lack of ability in the early stages prevents the student making responses in the later stages. The extracts below were used in an H.N.C. examination questions, and did not suffer greatly from this difficulty—it was in fact the easiest question on the paper, as judged by scores; about half of the students attempted it.

'. . . This number of valence electrons is accommodated by _____ hybridization, and the shape of the NO_2^- ion is therefore _____.
There are (is)_____ pair(s) of bonding electrons and _____ lone pair(s). The angle $\angle ONO$ will therefore be about _____ °.
We have now dealt with _____ -type covalent bonding and have yet to consider _____ -type covalency.

— —

These A.O.'s may combine to form a total of _____ M.O.'s. Assume that the A.O.'s are adding, but that arrangement of wave function signs varies, hence draw pictures (in the space below) of all these M.O.'s in terms of the A.O.'s from which they are composed:

Consider now, how these arrangements of signs will affect the bonding character of electrons in these M.O.'s. The numbers of bonding, non-bonding and antibonding M.O.'s will be respectively _____ , _____ and _____. Hence plot these, qualitatively, on an energy diagram, giving labels:

Place in these energy levels the number of available electrons deduced above.'

A similar question on the Jahn-Teller theorem has also been used at H.N.C. level. These choices of topic were made to ensure that the problem would involve abilities in the 'application' rather than 'knowledge' category. There are similarities between this type of question and the structured question discussed below. It may be possible to use the programmed type of question to measure students' abilities to learn, rather than abilities they have learned.

There are numerous disadvantages to the short-answer type of item:
  (i)   it is difficult to avoid ambiguity;
  (ii) students may spell wrongly or write illegibly;
  (iii) use of clues such as an indefinite article 'a' or 'an' must be avoided; this complicates the writing of items;
  (iv) the units and degree of precision must be indicated for numerical answers.

(b) Fixed-response items, sometimes called multiple-choice questions—although this is only the simplest type of such items. Here the student selects the correct answer from a list of alternatives. The range of abilities assessable by such items goes far beyond the simple recall or recognition of information, to include some of the higher orders of Bloom's (cognitive) taxonomy. The main types of item are:

(i)   Multiple Choice—there is only one correct response, the other three or four are 'distractors'.

(ii) True/False—a variant of multiple choice in which there are only two responses 'true' or 'false'.

(iii) Multiple Completion (multiple response)—several of the list of responses are correct; the student selects the correct combination.

(iv) Situation—the student is given a diagram, some data or the description of an experiment; he answers several multiple-choice items relating to this one situation.

(v)   Matching (classification)—two lists are provided: one of questions, another of possible responses. The student matches the two lists. Some responses may not be used, others may be used several times.

(vi) Assertion/Reason—an assertion (statement) is given, and also a possible reason (explanation); the student must decide whether each are individually correct, and if so whether the 'reason' does in fact explain the 'assertion'.

In each case, the item consists usually of a 'stem' posing the question and a set of possible responses ('options', 'alternatives') from which to choose. The correct response (or combination of responses) is called 'the key' and the incorrect responses are 'distractors'. Some examples of each type of item are given below:

1. *Multiple Choice*

Which one of the following is the correct description of products of the thermal decomposition of KIF_6
(a) KI and $3F_2$;
(b) KIF_2 and $2F_2$;
(c) KIF_4 and F_2;
(d) KF and IF_5.
Which of the following physical quantities are related directly by De Broglie's equation:
(a)   energy and mass;
(b)   energy and frequency;
(c)   wavelength and momentum;
(d)   momentum and position.

The first of these was used to assess the ability to *apply* the understanding of lattice energy, and is therefore an example of an item relating to high order educational objectives. The second example falls into the 'knowledge' category.

2. *True/False*

The molar free energy of a liquid is greater than that of its solid at any temperature below the melting point. Is this statement true or false?

This was probably designed as a 'comprehension' item, but might be answered on the basis of knowledge alone. In cases where the classification of an item is in doubt, perhaps because it involves several abilities, it is usual to use the highest order category.

3. *Multiple Completion*

Decide which of the responses is (are) correct and then choose
(*a*)   if only (i), (ii) and (iii) are correct;
(*b*)   if only (i) and (iii) are correct;
(*c*)   if only (ii) and (iv) are correct;
(*d*)   if only (iv) is correct.
The formation of ionic compounds is favoured by numerically low values for:
(i)   the ionization energy of the cation-forming element;
(ii)   the electron affinity of the anion-forming element;
(iii)   the sublimation energy of the cation-forming element;
(iv)   the lattice energy.

This type of question is similar to the use of a response array in the structural communication type of learning programme (*see* Chap. 11, where an example is given). The Open University Science Foundation Course has used multiple completion questions with as many as 49 alternative answers, in the form of a response array, from which to select a combination.[4] The marking of such complicated items is in this case handled by a computer (computer marked assignment).

4. *Situations*

Answer the following questions about the given Born-Haber cycle for NaCl. (Units are kJ mol^{-1})

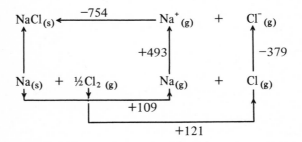

1.   Calculate the omitted quantity. The value is: (*a*) +348; (*b*) −1396; (*c*) −410; (*d*) +410.
2.   This quantity is called the:
(*a*)   lattice energy;
(*b*)   polarizability;
(*c*)   heat of dissociation;
(*d*)   heat of formation.
3.   One of the quantities can only be obtained by calculation (or by the use of the cycle); this is the:
(*a*)   electron affinity;
(*b*)   ionization energy;
(*c*)   lattice energy;
(*d*)   heat of formation.

4. Apart from this, the most difficult quantity to determine experimentally, is the:
   (a) heat of sublimation;
   (b) electron affinity;
   (c) heat of dissociation;
   (d) ionization energy.

5. *Matching*

Choose one of the answers (a)-(b) in response to each of the items (i)-(iii). Each answer may be used once, more than once or not at all.

$$(a)\ O_2^+;\ (b)\ O_2^-;\ (c)\ O_2\ ;\ (d)\ O_2^{2-}$$

(i) which is diamagnetic?
(ii) which has *two* unpaired electrons?
(iii) which has the longest bond?

Structured questions may be of this type. The one below is taken from a specimen London 'A' level paper.

(a) Below are given the names of five different compounds. In each case give the structural formula:
A. Methyl-buta-1,3-diene;
B. 3-Chloro-pentan-2,4-diol;
C. 2,2,4-Trimethyl-pentane;
D. *para*-Amino-benzoic acid;
E. 4-Iodo-2-methyl-pentan-1-ol;
(b)
   (i) Which one of the above compounds contains a group which is readily oxidized to form an acid?
   (ii) What reagent and conditions would you employ for this oxidation?
   (iii) Give the structural formula and the name of the acid formed;
(c)
   (i) Which of the above compounds would be the most likely starting material for a polymerization process?
   (ii) Briefly state your reasons for your answer;
   (iii) Give the structural arrangement of a part of the polymer chain which you would expect to be formed;
(d) Suppose you were given unlabelled samples of compounds B and E. Indicate how you would distinguish between them, using chemical tests only.

The question below is, in fact, taken from an Oral Examination at C.S.E. level.[5] It shows how fixed-response questions may be related to practical work.

Q5. We have seven different solutions and seven labels but we do not know which labels belong to which bottles. The tubes in front of each bottle all contain the solution from that bottle. *Illustrate by pointing to tubes in front of a particular bottle.* Before I do anything, can you put one label in place?

I am now going to do a number of tests on these solutions and after each test I want you to move one or more labels. The object is to label the bottles correctly.

| | E | J | K | H | L | A | M | |
	HCl	Na₂SO₄	Ca(NO₃)₂	H₂SO₄	NaNO₃	NaOH	CoCl₂	
Observation	—	—	—	—	—	—	—	....
$CuSO_4$	—	—	—	—	—	PPT	▨	....
Mg	GAS	—	—	GAS	—	▨	▨	....
$AgNO_3$	PPT			—		▨	▨	....
Na_2CO_3	▨	—	PPT	▨	—	▨	▨	....
$BaCl_2$	▨	PPT	▨	▨	—	▨	▨	....

6. *Assertion/Reason*

For the following questions, consider the two statements and select:
   (*a*) if both are true *and* (ii) is the explanation of (i);
   (*b*) if both are true but (ii) is *not* the explanation of (i);
   (*c*) if (i) is true *but* (ii) is false;
   (*d*) if (i) is *false* but (ii) is true.

Assertion	*Reason*
1. (i) Gamma radiation is not easily detected using a cloud chamber.	(ii) Neutrons are electrically uncharged.
2. (i) BF_3 is a good catalyst in aqueous solution for many reactions.	(ii) BF_3 is hydrolysed by water to give boric acid and HF only.

The Open University Science Foundation Course also uses a type of item referred to as 'ordering'. The student is asked to put up to seven items in a rank order according to a given criterion.

Other examples of questions are given by Dunning[6] and by Johnstone and Sharp.[7]

SCORING ITEMS

Multiple choice items are usually scored simply by giving a positive mark for the correct answer, and zero for incorrect answers. Guessing is thereby *not* penalized. A variation is to give a negative mark for incorrect answers such that random guessing would yield a total mark of zero over the whole test. The advantages of penalizing for guessing have often been debated[1,3] and the consensus seems to be that it is pointless to penalize since the overall rank order of candidates is unaltered. However, such comparisons have usually been poorly organized, in that the students take the same test twice at different times, or a different test, or different groups of students take the same test. The preliminary results of a study, in which these faults were avoided, indicate[8] that previous conclusions were over-simplifications. Penalization is usually necessary for a true/false item.

The Open University adopts a variety of scoring methods for multiple choice items.[9] These allow for some answers to be correct but not preferred, or for 'don't know' responses. Thus the preferred answer scores +1, the non-preferred answer scores 0, the penalized answer scores $-½$ and 'don't know' scores 0 or $1/x$ (x = number of alternatives). The possibility of a postive score for 'don't know' reflects the type of question in which the student is expected to realize that there is insufficient data to reach a conclusion. It is also possible to grade the preferred answers. A further variation is to take into account the confidence weighting, illustrated in the specimen examination question (above) on social implications. There are no penalty scores in this case. The student is always told when the confidence weighting will be taken into account. If he says he is certain when he gets an incorrect answer, he loses more marks than if he says he is uncertain. In many social situations uncertainty in answering would be expected in view of the lack of conclusive evidence.

In the array type of question, each item may be given a score of +2, +1, 0, −1 or −2. The student score is based upon a 'coherence index' which reflects the difference between the proportions of positive and negative items selected by the student. Other multiple completion items are scored as multiple choice.

In the 'matching' question, the preferred match may score +1, while the non-preferred match scores 0, the penalized match scores −½ and 'don't know' scores $1/y$ (y = number of items in second list).

The situation set of items is usually scored as a number of multiple choice questions. The assertion/reason question is usually scored as for multiple choice items; however, there is a case for giving more marks for those items which require a decision about the links between 'reason' and 'assertion' as well as a decision about the truth of each statement.

There are three different scoring options for 'ordering' questions: (i) only correct order throughout scores, (ii) each correctly ordered item scores and individual items can be weighted, or (ii) each correctly ordered item scores and items displaced only one position score something.

RELATIVE ADVANTAGES AND DISADVANTAGES OF EACH TYPE OF FIXED RESPONSE ITEM

Item	Advantages	Disadvantages
Multiple choice	Simplicity Large numbers of distractors reduce chances of guessing; students not exposed to any false statements; applicable to branched learning programmes and other feedback	Often impossible to think of four or five *plausible* distractors; sometimes two or more alternatives may be correct, depending on the sophistication of the student
True/false	Simplicity; some statements can only be written with two rather than five alternatives	Too easy to guess, so this must be penalized; few areas are so clear-cut that there is no alternative besides 'true' and 'false'; student exposed to false statements
Multiple completion	Easy to construct since several correct answers are permitted; few incorrect distractors need to be constructed; no false statements	Instructions to students are complicated

Situation	Comprehension, application and evaluation can be easily tested; relationships between areas can be made by connecting items to a common situation	Difficult to think of situations which are not too similar to those the student has encountered, and yet which he has enough knowledge and ability to answer; complex to construct
Matching	Comprehension can be easily tested; related areas can be brought together; few distractors per item since one list serves several items	Complex to construct; instructions are complicated; all responses must be homogeneous in being related in some way; gives false impression of clear distinctions between categories (e.g. of material, properties, interactions)
Assertion/Reason	Reasoning ability is easily tested; large numbers of distractors unnecessary	Students exposed to false statements; instructions are complicated; difficult to ensure that a 'reason' is either completely false at all levels of sophistication, or is *uniquely* correct

ADVANTAGES AND DISADVANTAGES OF FIXED-RESPONSE TESTS COMPARED WITH OTHER METHODS OF ASSESSMENT[2]

Advantages	Disadvantages
Reliable;	Do not assess attitudes or creativity;
Cover large areas of syllabus;	Syllabuses may not be common to all students tested;
Student spends more time thinking than writing;	Do not assess ability to organize and state coherently;
Easy to mark;	Difficult to construct;
Testing characterizes each item's usefulness;	Need to be tested and to involve a team;
Easily related to stated aims which can be given to students;	Cannot be used in open-ended situations;
Allows course or learning package to be evaluated;	
Easy and exact feedback to student;	Need to keep items secure;
Compulsory, so that non-equivalent options do not arise;	Do not cater for student's interests or individuality;
Particularly useful in testing for attainment of knowledge;	Stress recognition rather than recall of knowledge;
Can be used to assess most cognitive abilities;	Too easy to emphasize lower orders since higher order items very difficult to construct;
Desired mix of levels of difficulty and types of objective selected in advance	

This list shows that objective and traditional tests nicely complement each other. An assessment procedure should therefore use a mixture of all techniques, since each measures different types of ability. More detailed information about each student's abilities should be derived from such a designed assessment.

The necessity for stating objectives clearly has emphasized the abilities which fixed-response questions can assess. However, if other methods of assessment are to be used to their maximum advantage in a complementary way, it is essential to design them with similar care. Now that objective tests are becoming accepted, perhaps groups of chemists should turn their efforts towards realizing the full potential of essay questions.

FUNCTIONS OF ASSESSMENT[2,10]

Objective tests may be used to—
  (*a*) test the attainment of students in specified abilities;
  (*b*) select students for other courses or employment (prediction);
  (*c*) provide feedback to the student on his own progress;
  (*d*) provide feedback to student's counsellor;
  (*e*) evaluate the effectiveness of a course, lecture, film, learning programme etc.;
  (*f*) provide information whether objectives can be attained, and therefore whether they need modifying;
  (*g*) provide information on whether the attainment of specified objectives produces students who are successful in employment;
  (*h*) motivate the student to learn, and reinforce this learning by knowledge of results.

The first two functions concern the main uses of assessment—to check mastery in the hope that all students score 100 per cent; and to discriminate to the maximum extent among students.

The diagnostic uses of assessment are not well developed. However, the 'feedback classroom', used by Hollings and Whitworth at Chesterfield College of Technology (H.N.C. level) and by Glynn at Chelsea,[11] utilizes a number of multiple choice questions to check the understanding of lectures in progress. Elton has developed the use of matching items to provide a 'pre-knowledge test' for physics courses,[12] (*see* Chap. 10).

Little systematic work has been devoted to the use of assessment data in order to evaluate the effectiveness of courses. However, the Open University courses are designed to be evaluated in this way. The validation of learning programmes is a smaller scale illustration of the same course evaluation process (*see* Chap. 11).

The affect of the assessment scheme itself, on the course and on the student, must be considered. The assessment process should be seen as a vital part of the learning activities of the student.

CONSTRUCTING FIXED-RESPONSE TESTS

The essential step in constructing an assessment item is to relate it to a specific objective. Once the aims of the course have been decided, and described by detailed objectives (*see* Chap. 3), the assessment scheme can be constructed. This process was described in Chap. 11, since it is closely related to the design of criterion tests for learning programmes. However, the assessment scheme has functions beyond testing for the achievement of specified abilities. As described in the last section, the test may be designed to check students' mastery of certain abilities ('criterion reference'), or to differentiate amongst students with a view to predicting their later performance ('norm reference'). This will affect the construction of assessment items since questions which might be adequate in a criterion test, could be too facile to discriminate students.

In constructing the items, it is necessary to ensure that some worthwhile and relevant ability is being tested. Thus if the student has only been memorizing a piece of knowledge in his course, it may be foolish to expect him to use it at the 'application' level in a test. Further, if the objective specifies certain acts (such as recording a spectrum) and conditions (such as the laboratory), it cannot be tested by asking the student to make a written response in an examination room.

A useful way of designing a test is to decide what emphasis is to be given to each of the categories of objective. Thus, in the R.I.C. scheme for first-year university and H.N.C. tests in inorganic chemistry, the aim was for 30 per cent 'knowledge' items, 30 per cent 'comprehension' items and 40 per cent 'higher level' items. Further it was decided to aim at an even spread over the syllabus sections, and levels of difficulty and the inclusion of a reasonable number of types of item (35% multiple choice, 30% multiple completion, 2½% match, 2½% situation and 30% assertion/reason). For this purpose a grid may be constructed specifying the item type, syllabus section, ability and facility desired for each item.

The items are constructed to fit the specification, but this process is largely pragmatic. The only rule is to avoid the common faults discussed below, but these cannot sometimes be seen until the item has been written down and criticized by several people.

At this stage, the writer's ideas about the characteristics of each item form the basis for the test construction. These may be modified by the detailed criticism and improvements derived from other members of the test construction team ('shredding'). However, trials of the test-paper with students are the only sure way of accurately characterizing each item. It is therefore necessary to construct more items than are needed, in order to allow for a selection to be made after trials which will meet the test specification.

Strict adherence to the grid is rather pedantic, and in any case the specification of item type is of no significance beyond ensuring variety in the test format. A good case can be made for specifying abilities, related subject areas and standards of the question—these are usually part of the statement of the objective. While some types of objective might relate best to a particular item type (e.g. situation—evaluation, assertion/reason—analysis, array—organization of concepts), the choice of item type is generally peripheral. The choice may be made to suit a particular subject content, which for example might be unsuited to questions with uniquely correct answers. A more useful approach, than specifying the item type on a grid, might be to write all items as multiple choice questions unless this would distort the objective. Whitfield,[13] Mathews,[14] Fensham[15] and Dunning[6] have also discussed schemes for the construction of test papers.

THE ELIMINATION OF COMMON FAULTS IN ITEMS

Parameters

Once constructed and criticized by colleagues, all items must be tried out on a large number of students (~250). Analysis of the test data yields several characteristics.[1,3]

(i)   Reliability of the test as a whole. This measures the consistency from item to item as a correlation coefficient, either between two sittings of the test or between randomly split halves of the same test. Various formulae have been given.

(ii)   The facility index is the percentage of total students who correctly answered an individual item. Those of medium difficulty are said to fall between 30 and 70 per cent.

(iii)   The discrimination index is a measure of the power of an item to discriminate between students of different abilities. A number of formulae have been used, the simplest being:

$$\frac{(H - L)}{N}$$

where H = number of students in top half who answered the item correctly.
L = number of students in bottom half who answered the item correctly.
N = number of students in each half.

Here, the top and bottom halves are determined by the rank order for the whole test.

More refined formulae used the top and bottom thirds, or 27 per cent. The index varies between -1 and $+1$, values above $+0\cdot3$ usually being considered acceptable.

(iv)   Effectiveness of the distractors, in terms of the percentage of responses attracted by each alternative.

An unreliable test (correlation $<0\cdot5$) would have to be reconstructed with fresh items. However, usually the test as a whole is reliable, the various indices revealing that certain items should be rejected or modified. The most useful characteristics are the facility index and the effectiveness of distractors. Usually items with facility indices between 10 and 90 per cent can be used, but items which virtually all students or no students answer correctly are useless *for assessing students.* They may have important uses in evaluating courses or learning programmes or for feedback to students. Normally, the test will aim to include a balanced selection of relatively easy, difficult and average items. Hence it is useful to know the facility index of each item.

If two distractors attract no response, a four-choice item is effectively only a two choice item, and should be rejected:

	Good Item					*Poor Item*		
A*	B	C	D		A	B	C*	D
50%	16	17	17		3	15	80	2

(*marks the correct response)

The discrimination index is of dubious value. One well-known guide to objective testing states:[3]

"It is possible to have a negative index of discrimination, i.e. the correct choice has been selected more frequently by 'poor candidates' than by 'good candidates.' Such items should be eliminated at the pre-test stage."

However, such an item has detected an ability possessed by one group of students, they do not happen to have as many other abilities as the 'top' group of students. If the item is then eliminated, we remove this ability from those being assessed, and discriminate still further against the 'bottom' group of students.

Moreover, the students are defined as 'top' or 'bottom' solely on the basis of this test; removing items of negative discrimination self-perpetuates any faults in the validity of the test. The assumption implicit in the quotation above is that students will have many abilities or none; and that if we find just one ability, the test must be wrong. This is not far removed from expecting that students' answers to essay questions, objective tests, project work and all other methods of assessments should necessarily correlate highly. If this were the case, the effort involved in using several methods of assessment together, is wasted. Three possible ways to use the discrimination index are:

1.   Ignore this information, and modify items only on basis of other data.

2.   Look carefully at items of negative discrimination. Is there something obviously wrong with them? If not, what ability is being tested? Is this useful and can we write more such items? Collect information on all items of negative discrimination. (Reject items of very low positive discrimination, or -0.3 to $+0.3$).

3.   Make analysis of test data as sophisticated as the design of the items by relating them to categories of objective. Thus, analyse all the items of the same ability type together to give discrimination indices for each item *relative to other items of the same ability type.*

If nothing is obviously wrong with the item, then strategy 3 would appear to make best use of the available information; this may only be possible when the test contains many items, such that there are a significant number of each ability type. The logical extension of this course of action would be to perform a factor analysis on the test data, in order to isolate factors representing the characteristics of the items, *as seen by the students.* The item writer's idea of an 'application' item may not be the same as the students'. Such a factor analysis is being carried out, but runs the risk that the final factors may be content-dependent rather than ability-dependent.

Common faults in items are:[1,3]

(*a*)   Several correct answers where one is intended;

(*b*)   Ambiguity in meaning of stem and options;

(*c*)   Problem not stated clearly in a positive form and with brevity;

(*d*)   Options not parallel in construction or content;

(*e*)   Answers given away by wording, construction, length, text-book phraseology, or detail;

(*f*)   Nothing worthwhile is being tested;

(*g*)   Absolute terms included in distractors—'always', 'never', 'all' etc., are usually known to be false;

(*h*)   Two (or more) distractors have the same meaning and can therefore not both be correct in a multiple choice item, therefore they must both be wrong;

(*i*)   Use of two responses which together are all inclusive, eliminates the rest,

(*j*)   Inhomogeneous material in matching items;

(*k*)   Not all distractors are plausible;

(*l*)   Items not independent;

(*m*)   An application type of item which is of standard kind and therefore not new to the student.

Some examples of these faults are given below for multiple choice items. Daniels[16] gives further examples. The examples are at secondary level.

    1.   Which of the following electromagnetic radiations is most important to us:
    A.   X-rays;
    B.   Visible light;
    C.   Radio waves;
    D.   Ultra-violet;
    E.   Infra-red.

Since the item does not specify in what respect 'important' is to be construed, the student would be correct in giving any answer.

    2.   A convex lens of focal length 10 cm forms an image of an object placed 20 cm from the lens. The image will be:
    A.   real and erect;
    B.   twice as long as the object;
    C.   on the opposite side of the lens to the object;
    D.   smaller than the object;
    E.   virtual.

In this case, responses (C) and (E) together include all situations and therefore the other distractors are superfluous. However, it can be argued that the student must understand as much optics to appreciate this as to answer the question in a straight-forward manner.

    3.   The density of ice is 0.9 cm^{-3}, and of water is 1g cm^{-3}. The *change* in volume when 1g of ice melts is (in cm^3):
    A.   a decrease of $(1-0.9)$;
    B.   an increase of $(1-0.9)$;
    C.   a decrease of $(\frac{1}{1}-\frac{1}{0.9})$
    D.   an increase of $(\frac{1}{1}-\frac{1}{0.9})$;
    E.   a decrease of $(\frac{1}{0.9}-\frac{1}{1})$.

In this case, (D) and (E) are equivalent, and must therefore both be incorrect; the item then reduced to one of three choices. It has been argued that the student must be capable of logical reasoning before he can answer such a question in this way, and that the ability to reason logically is a valuable one such that the item is still useful. However, this argument ignores the fact that the question may be answered without the ability it was designed to measure, because it is accidentally possible to answer it using a different ability. If the different ability is desirable, it should be included in the objectives anyway; the problem of writing an item to fit the intended ability still remains.

    4.   A ray of white light passes through a prism and is refracted at both surfaces. Which of the following statements is FALSE:
    A.   the emergent ray is coloured;
    B.   the ray is deviated;
    C.   dispersion occurs;
    D.   the red light is refracted least;
    E.   the red light is slowed down most.

In this case, some light must be red, since (D) and (E) cannot *both* be false. Hence, (A), (B) and (C) must both be true, since dispersion is the process producing colour and it involves differential deviation. Hence, the item is one of only two choices (D) or (E).

IMPROVEMENT OF ITEMS

Items can often be improved by re-writing as a different type. Thus, in its original
format, the situation question about the NaCl Born-Haber cycle consisted of one
multiple-choice question. However, this required the inspection of six pieces of data to
find which had the incorrect sign (or six calculations without any knowledge) plus the
naming of this quantity. Such an effort is better spread over more than one item, and
so the situation format was adopted. Some other examples of the modification of
unsatisfactory multiple-choice items are given below:

Example 1

Multiple Choice

Schrödinger developed an equation, the solutions of which are:
  A.   potential energies;
  B.   orbitals;
  C.   wavefunctions alone;
  D.   wavefunctions and corresponding total energies.
The correct answer is much longer than the rest and is of a different construction

Multiple Completion

The solutions of Schrödinger's wave equation are:
  (i)   potential energies;
  (ii)   total energies;
  (iii) quantum numbers;
  (iv)   wavefunctions.

Example 2

Multiple Choice

Crystals may diffract:
  A.   X-rays, electrons and neutrons;
  B.   X-rays and electrons, but not neutrons;
  C.   Electrons and neutrons, but not X-rays;
  D.   X-rays only.
This is cumbersome.

Multiple Completion

Crystals may diffract:
  (i)   X-rays;
  (ii)   electrons;
  (iii) neutrons;
  (iv) α-rays.

Example 3

Multiple Choice

The thermal stabilities and acid strengths of HF and HCl are as follows:
   A.   HCl is more stable, but less acidic than HF;
   B.   HCl is more stable, and more acidic than HF;
   C.   HCl is less stable, and less acidic than HF;
   D.   HCl is less stable, but more acidic than HF;
   This is a cumbersome way of checking whether the student understands the main determinants of acid strength. and also requires him to answer two two-choice items posing as one question.

Assertion/Reason

Assertion	*Reason*
HF is a stronger acid than HCl	F is more electro- negative than Cl.

Example 4

Multiple Choice

That 4s fills before 3d, when adding electrons to build up the periodic table, is due to:
   A.   the convergence of all energy levels as n increases;
   B.   The presence of less electron density close to the nucleus for the 3d orbital compared with 4s;
   C.   the lanthanide contraction;
   D.   the Zeeman effect.
   In this case, (C) and (D) are not plausible distractors and the correct answer is longer and more specific than the rest.

Assertion/Reason

Assertion	*Reason*
When the aufbau principle is applied in building up the periodic table in terms of electronic configuration, electrons enter the 4s orbital before 3d.	The energy levels of the orbitals all converge as the principal quantum number increases.

References

1. Various papers in *Educ. Chem.* **6** (1969); H. G. Macintosh and R. B. Morrison, *Objective Testing,* University of London Press 1969; N. E. Gronlund, *Constructing Achievement Tests,* Prentice-Hall, New York 1968; R. L. Ebel, *Measuring Educational Achievement,* Prentice-Hall, New York 1969; R. L. Thorndike and F. Hagen, *Measurement and Evaluation in Psychology and Education,* Wiley, New York 1969.

2. R. Cox, *Univ. Quart.* **21**, 292 (1967); National Union of Students, *Executive Report on Examinations,* National Union of Students, London 1969; *Report of One Day Conference on Assessment,* National Union of Students, London 1970.
3. *Objective Testing,* City and Guilds of London Institute 1969.
4. Science Foundation Course, The Open University, Walton 1971.
5. P. Brown, P. J. Hitchman and G. D. Yeoman, *C.S.E. an Experiment in the Oral Examining of Chemistry,* Schools Council Examinations Bulletin 21, Evans/Methuen Education, London 1971.
6. G. M. Dunning, *Sci. Educ.* **38**, 191 (1954).
7. A. H. Johnstone and D. W. A. Sharp, *Chem. Brit.* **8**, 69 (1972).
8. D. E. Billing, unpublished work.
9. M. W. Neil, personal communication 1971.
10. A. N. Openheim, M. Jahoda and R. L. James, *Univ. Quart.* **21**, 341 (1967).
11. T. A. Whitworth, *School Sci. Rev.* **47**, 654 (1966); **48**, 721 (1967); E. Glynn, J. P. Pearce and A. S. Willott, in *Aspects of Educational Technology,* Vol. 4, A. C. Bajpai and J. F. Leedham (Eds.), Pitman, London 1970, p. 54; K. Holling, in *Media and Methods,* D. Unwin (Ed.), McGraw-Hill, London 1969.
12. S. O'Connell, A. W. Wilson and L. R. B. Elton, *Nature* **222**, 526 (1969).
13. R. C. Whitfield, *School Sci. Rev.* **52**, 23 (1969).
14. J. C. Mathews, *School Sci. Rev.* **49**, 2 (1967).
15. P. J. Fensham, *Australian Sci. Teachers J.* **20**, 103 (1969).
16. D. J. Daniels, *School Sci. Rev.* **50**, 19 (1969).

V. CONCLUSIONS

CHAPTER 17

Developments in Advanced Science Education

B. S. FURNISS

The upsurge of interest in science education in recent years has been remarkable. Taking chemical education as a particular example, we have seen the establishment of a division of the Chemical Society concerned entirely with education (with an anticipated membership of over 4,000), the foundation of a chair of chemical education (at the University of East Anglia) and the appointment of research fellows in chemical education at a number of universities and polytechnics. Further evidence of the wide interest is reflected in the flurry of meetings and conferences devoted to aspects of this topic, such as the three-day conference at Thames Polytechnic which attracted over 100 participants, and the inaugural meeting of the Education Division of the Chemical Society at which there were over 200 people. The purpose of this paper is not to attempt to analyse the causes of this development, but rather to survey the areas of interest, particularly as evidenced by the lectures and discussions at the Thames Polytechnic meeting.

AIMS AND OBJECTIVES

The majority of teachers are required to teach courses which they have not devised themselves and for which aims are defined (if at all) only in very general terms. The courses are controlled at a national, regional, faculty or departmental level and the establishment of a philosophy for a particular course is generally a fairly long term process. The criteria on which to base aims are obviously complex and are likely to be subject to considerable variation from one individual to another. In the past the aims have been determined by the subject matter and its interpretation by the teacher; the predominant influences have been academic, with little or no regard paid to either industry or society. We are now turning much more to a consideration of the needs and abilities of students as a source of the aims of courses.

Detailed objectives for particular sections of the course are usually left very much in the hands of the individual teacher and the explicit formulation of them is of value to the teacher since he should then be better able to select, on a rational basis, teaching and assessment methods appropriate to particular topics or lecture series. The actual process of formulating detailed objectives forces the teacher to clarify his thinking about his subject as a whole and about specific sections of it, and this in itself is likely to be of considerable value, possibly the most important outcome of the whole exercise. Once a list of objectives has been compiled it should, of course, be made available to students, so that they may derive maximum motivation and direction from it, and also to colleagues teaching other sections of the same course for information and criticism.

COURSES (curriculum)

The great emphasis on the acquisition and repetition of facts in many courses cannot be defended in view of the likely redundancy of that knowledge within the lifetime of the student. The balance between the knowledge, skills and attitudes components will vary between courses but it is important that the latter two receive the same kind of detailed consideration as the first. There is a danger that components (such as knowledge) which are relatively easily assessed and understood will receive inordinate attention, far beyond their merits, to the virtual exclusion of other areas such as interest and creativity, which are neglected simply because they are difficult to define and measure.

The change in employment patterns of pure science graduates necessitates a close examination of the type of knowledge, skills and attitudes which the courses are designed to encourage. Prof. Holliday[1] suggests new courses with a greater emphasis on 'relevance' and 'communication' and there is growing support for this view.

Of the many developments and innovations in tertiary science courses, the Open University courses probably represent the most radical break with tradition, but not only in the use of new teaching methods, which was necessitated by the nature of the student body; the use of the systems approach to course design, the detailed specification of objectives for each course unit, the provision of self assessment questions and conceptual diagrams relating units and topics within units, and the attempts to relate the pure science disciplines such as biology and chemistry to industry and society generally, are all features from which much can be learnt. A second course which offers a fundamentally new approach is the degree by thesis in chemistry at Sussex University. One of the dangers with this approach is that the graduates will have a substantial bias towards pure research, but this is not a great risk when balanced against the increased application and motivation likely to be developed by this type of student-centred approach. Prof. Eaborn's preliminary report[2] is encouraging but it is obviously too early to make any firm assessment of the experiment.

An alternative way of making pure science courses more 'relevant' is to link the study of the science subject with one or more of the social sciences. An example of this approach is the Technological Economics curriculum at Stirling, one section of which, the honours course in biology and economics is, broadly speaking, designed to equip an honours economist with general degree standard biology. Similar types of courses which link the study of a science subject with that of education are described by Roberts.[3] Although the graduates from these courses will not necessarily become teachers, the content and nature of these courses cannot be separated from the much discussed subject of the training of science teachers generally. The whole topic has been given vast publicity of late following the publication of the James Report and the report of the Royal Society.[4] Of particular relevance here is the assertion that[5] 'it is neither possible nor, in our view, desirable that more than a minority of our science teachers should have followed a specialized three year honours course of the usual type'. It is likely that there will be an increasing demand for teachers with an understanding of a broad range of science and its social implications, not just for elementary courses, but at the intellectual level suitable for sixth form courses.

EDUCATIONAL TECHNIQUES

In order for the teacher to select and use effectively the most appropriate means for achieving a given set of objectives, whether explicit or not, a number of requirements must be met. Firstly, he must be aware of the range of techniques which are available; secondly, he must be familiar with the scope and limitations of each method, thirdly, he must possess the expertise to use and modify new methods as necessary, and fourthly, he must be sufficiently flexible in his approach to teaching to modify his own teaching methods in the light of new developments and requirements. Unless these requirements are met it is unreasonable to expect much progress toward the general introduction of new techniques, and even where they are introduced, to look for unanimous approval. As Prof. Elton points out,[6] the introduction of radically new teaching methods needs to be very carefully prepared and controlled if antagonism from both fellow staff and students is to be avoided. Flood Page makes a similar point in his excellent monograph[7] devoted specifically to the question of the use of educational technology in higher education: 'much educational good can come of the proper use of what modern technology has to offer, but vast expenditure on machines is no guarantee of good education.' Significant developments in this area can only come from a clear definition of objectives from the individual teacher and a thorough appreciation of the various ways in which they may be achieved.

One characteristic commonly associated with programmed learning is that it allows the individual student to progress at his own pace through a given piece of work. Expansion of this idea of individualized instruction into a whole course (such as the Keller Plan described by Prof. Elton[8]) has been attempted at a number of American institutions.[9] The highly structured nature of science subjects makes it desirable (and often necessary) for a student to understand one topic before proceeding to the next, and this is precisely the requirement of the various types of individualized instruction methods. Such a system requires a rather low student to staff ratio; this problem has been overcome in America by using, for example, second year students to 'teach' first year students etc. However, the fall in the number of students in chemistry departments in polytechnics and universities in this country offers an ideal opportunity for similar experiments here, since low student-staff ratios are not uncommon.

An important factor in the modification of existing courses and the development of new courses and new teaching techniques is the large amount of time they demand from the individual teacher; frequently an individual cannot afford to devote as much time as he would like to this area due to pressure of other work. Better results could well be obtained if departments reorganized their timetables to allow individual teachers more time to work in these important areas.

ASSESSMENT

'A substantial number of teachers (in higher education) are relatively uncritical of traditional types of examinations.'[10] As a first step towards improving, where necessary, the existing assessment-procedures, it is useful to analyse the existing examinations as described, for example, by Mackaill.[15] Then consideration could be given, firstly, to whether the examination is fulfilling the functions it is supposed to be, and secondly, to whether there are any additional desirable objectives, such as the encouragement of particular working habits and attitudes, or course evaluation, which could be achieved by alternative assessment procedures and variation in the frequency of use. Further benefit is likely to result from attempting to relate the method of assessment (objective testing, open book, extended essay, project report, literature survey, continuous assessment etc.) to particular course objectives.

The treatment of the results of the various assessment procedures raises further problems. Typical current practice is to combine marks obtained from traditional examinations, projects and continuous assessment, giving arbitrary weighting to the various sections. The significance of the mark obtained by averaging measures of different abilities on different scales in arbitrary proportions is far from clear, and its value in predicting future performance in possibly unrelated tasks is debatable.

CONCLUSIONS

A recurring theme has been the need to change the emphasis in Science education from the acquisition of knowledge towards a development of skills and attitudes which will, it is hoped, be of value to the student throughout his life and will not become redundant as will much of the knowledge that we use a vehicle for this process. Since the majority of teachers in advanced science education did not have the benefit of this enlightened attitude to their own education it is possible that their willingness to accept change will be somewhat less than the students they teach. It is likely that this basic conservatism of the existing teachers in further and higher science education is, and will continue to be, one of the major barriers in the acceptance of a continuously changing system of education. As the late Sir Ronald Nyholm[11] pointed out 'Man will accept change but he needs to be educated to do so. We can't slow down the world, but at least we can try to ensure that fewer people want to get off. Only the right kind of education will achieve this.' This is equally relevant for the teachers as for those they teach. Much attention has been given to the training of secondary teachers but comparatively little to that of teachers in further and higher education (only 5 of the 133 recommendations of the James Committee were concerned with F.E. teachers). Some universities and polytechnics are experimenting with short, voluntary training induction courses[12] for new teaching staff, these must become the rule rather than the exception and in due course should be supplemented by refresher courses for existing staff.

The continued expansion of higher science education is likely to result in a swing away from specialism. There can surely be no justification for increasing the production of graduates, highly specialized in a single discipline, with no career prospects in their chosen field. But the development of combined, integrated or joint degree courses must not result in a watered-down survey type of science course which only scratches the surface of the subject. Epstein has described a novel approach[13] which was developed for teaching science to non-science majors; it is largely based on the idea that science is what scientists do, which is not necessarily the same as what appears in science textbooks. The development of important concepts is traced through a series of research papers which are read in detail; the scheme has many merits, but in particular the important role of experimentation in science is continually emphasized and it is this facet of the subject which can too easily be overlooked in more traditional courses.

The structure and nature of pure science courses has resulted largely from the historical development of the subjects. Only recently have attempts[14] been made to analyse the conceptual and intellectual requirements of various parts of a subject and to relate these to the intellectual development of the student. Too often is the student presented with some of the conceptually most difficult material in his first term of higher education, the time when he is probably least able to cope with it. With the continual development of new courses and especially science courses where entry requirements differ from the traditional science A-level passes, more and detailed work in this area is urgently needed.

References

1. A. K. Holliday, in *Aims, Methods and Assessment in Advanced Science Education,* D. E. Billing and B. S. Furniss (Eds.), Heyden & Son, London 1973, p. 000 (this volume).
2. C. Eaborn, in *Aims, Methods and Assessment in Advanced Science Education,* D. E. Billing and B. S. Furniss (Eds.), Heyden & Son, London 1973, p. 000 (this volume).
3. I. F. Roberts, in *Aims, Methods and Assessment in Advanced Science Education,* D. E. Billing and B. S. Furniss (Eds.), Heyden & Son, London 1973, p. 000 (this volume).
4. *The Training of Teachers of Science and Mathematics,* The Royal Society, London 1972.
5. *The Training of Teachers of Science and Mathematics,* The Royal Society, London 1972, p. 5.
6. L. R. B. Elton, in *Aims, Methods and Assessment in Advanced Science Education,* D. E. Billing and B. S. Furniss (Eds.), Heyden & Son, London 1973, p. 000 (this volume).
7. C. Flood Page, *Technical Aids to Teaching in Higher Education,* Society for Research into Higher Education, London 1971, p. 4.
8. L. R. B. Elton, in *Aims, Methods and Assessment in Advanced Science Education,* D. E. Billing and B. S. Furniss (Eds.), Heyden & Son, London 1973, p. 000 (this volume).
9. B. V. Koen and F. S. Keller (for example), *Eng. Educ.* **61**, 504 (1971).
10. R. M. Beard and D. A. Bligh, *Research into Teaching Methods in Higher Education* 3rd Edn., Society for Research into Higher Education, London 1971, p. 63.
11. R. S. Nyholm, *J. Chem. Educ.* **48**, 34 (1971).
12. H. Greenaway, *Training of University Teachers,* Society for Research into Higher Education, London 1971.

13. H. T. Epstein, *A Strategy for Education,* Oxford University Press 1970; *Nature* **235**, 203 (1972).
14. (*a*) A. H. Johnstone, T. I. Morrison and D. W. A. Sharp, *Educ. Chem.* **8**, 212 (1971); (*b*) R. B. Ingle and M. Shayer, *Educ. Chem.* **8**, 182 (1971).
15. A. W. Mackaill, in *Aims, Methods and Assessment in Advanced Science Education,* D. E. Billing and B. S. Furniss (Eds.), Heyden & Son, London 1973, p. 000 (this volume).

VI. APPENDICES

APPENDIX A

A Glossary of Some Educational Terms

D. BILLING

Aim. The overall purpose or desired goal of a course or part of a course. Often not possible to define exactly, except in terms of a large number of detailed objectives (q.v.). To be distinguished from objective by virtue of detail and short-term nature of the latter.

Algorithm. Set of explicit instructions usually set out in terms of a flow-diagram with decision points.

Analysis. The breaking down of a complex problem in order to synthesize a solution; 1. This is one type of intellectual ability, included in some classifications (e.g. Bloom's); 2. A method of facilitating training by the detailed study of a master performer (q.v.). Results presented as networks. **A**. *Task Analysis:* A complex operation (job) consists of a number of tasks. If these tasks and their interrelation are identified, a task analysis has been completed. **B**. *Skills Analysis:* A task has a number of skills which need to be organized and coordinated in order to carry out the task successfully. The identification of these skills is called 'skills analysis'. **C**. *Behavioural Analysis:* Analysis of desired behaviour in terms of stimulus-response (q.v.) connections.

Attitude. (Mental)   A pre-disposition to behave in certain ways.

Behaviour.   **A**. The response made to some stimuli, the response itself being simple or complex, overt (observable) or covert (not apparent, e.g. thinking).   **B**. *Terminal behaviour:* desired behaviour resulting from learning.

Branching. A type of learning programme (q.v.) in which the answers to questions determine the sequence in which the remainder of the programme is tackled.

Chain. A series of responses. Each response contains some element which is a stimulus for the next response. One component of a behavioural analysis diagram.

Cognitive. Related to thinking, reasoning and intellectual abilities.

Communication. The process underlying teaching, training, educating, instructing, demonstrating, persuading, advertising, etc. Passing on of information.

Conditioning. **A**. *Classical conditioning* (Pavlovian): A response such as blinking the eyes (when the stimulus of a puff of air is directed at the cornea) becomes associated with an unnatural (conditioned) stimulus such as an audible click. Involuntary.	**B.** *Operant conditioning* (Skinnerian)' An operation (operant = stimulus and its response) is performed voluntarily because it achieves a goal. The goal has been determined by the instructor.

Criterion Test. Test designed to measure the degree to which a learning programme (q.v.) attains its objectives (q.v.).

Cue. (cf. 'prompt') As in the theatrical sense, used to indicate a stimulus which initiates activity such as solving a problem.

Cybernetics. The study of automatic machines and control systems for such machines. Relates the way in which they work to the way in which the brain is thought to function.

Discrimination.	**A.** One of the elements into which skills are analysed—e.g. it is necessary to discriminate between a conical flask and a beaker before a recrystallization is carried out. They are distinguished by looking for dissimilar features.	**B.** An index of the power of a test item to differentiate candidates who do well or badly on the test as a whole.

Distractor. All the possible responses to a question except the correct one. Sometimes incorrectly used to refer to all the responses (alternative answers).

Domain. A division of objectives (q.v.). Usually used with Bloom's classification of abilities into three areas (domains).	**A.** *Cognitive domain*—thinking, reasoning, recalling.	**B.** *Affective domain*—attitude to values; feelings, interests.	**C.** *Psychomotor domain*—manual skills, manipulation, muscular coordination.

Entry test. A test to check that certain skills, knowledge etc., required to start a learning programme, are already in the repertoire of the student (contrast 'pre-test').

Educational Technology. 'The development, application and evaluation of the systems, techniques and aids to improve the process of human learning' (NCET).

Evaluation.	**A.** The determination of the degree to which the educational objectives have been achieved. To be distinguished from 'assessment' which characterizes the student's attainment rather than that of the course, lecture or other learning 'package'.	**B.** An ability involving judgement with given criteria.

Extrinsic.	**A.** Linear learning programme in which the sequence the student takes is determined externally by the writer.	**B.** Motivation (incentive) provided by threat of failing examinations, punishment, reward etc.

Facility. An index of the ease with which students tackled a test item. The percentage of candidates who correctly answered the item.

Feedback.	**A.** In teaching, training and self-instructional material, feedback means knowledge of results (KR).	**B.** Feedback to the producer of material, via a trial, enables him to revise and improve.	**C.** Feedback to the learner by confirming or correcting his responses allows him to adjust and adapt (i.e. his behaviour is shaped to that required by the environment).

Frame. A small step or unit in a learning programme (q.v.), consisting of some information and a question relating to it. The name derives from the open window in teaching machines, through which the information is seen.

Frames in linear programmes usually require a response constructed by the student in answer to the question. A teaching sequence of from 3 to 8 frames is normally ended by a 'key' (or 'terminal') frame which tests the concept.

In branching programmes, frames contain 2-5 possible answers which the student selects after reading the frame. The choice made determines the next frame seen.

Generalization. A stimulus-response link (e.g. red light, therefore do not cross the road) may become generalized so that more than one stimulus (e.g. a green flashing light or a continuous red light) produces the same response. This is another element in a behavioural analysis network.

Hardware. A piece of equipment, e.g. computers, projectors, teaching machines, videotape recorder, camera etc., designed to operate with fixed medium.

Heuristic. An approach which emphasizes that much learning occurs by discovery and encourages this by providing a structured series of problematic situations. Emphasized by the 'Gestalt' school of psychologists who consider that learning involves sudden flashes of insight. Neglected by the other main school of psychologists who concentrate on shaping behaviour without reference to such internal processes as thinking or feeling.

Intrinsic. A. Branching learning programme in which the sequence the student follows is determined internally by his answers to questions. B. Motivation provided by the subject matter itself.

Item. Often used instead of 'question' since many are not direct questions but completions of statements etc. Component of a test.

Job Description. (Job Specification) A series of tasks which may or may not be related, together with details covering responsibilities, authority, qualifications, skills and personal qualities required for an occupation.

Key. The correct response to a question (item) in a test.

Knowledge. Facts, concepts or theories possessed by a person.

Learning. The forming or changing of behaviour, as a result of acquiring a mental or physical skill or an attitude.

Learning Experience. Everyone lives and works in a variety of environments. In order to prepare a person for a working environment it is necessary to analyse that environment not only for the skills, qualities, etc. required, but also for other factors that he will experience, e.g. noise, stress etc. A learning experience is then designed to train a person in a real (or substitute) environment.

A learning experience consists of 1. The programme (not necessarily *a* programme) or 'package' of essential activities; 2. Operational environment factors (other than the essential activities). The factors in the situation which help the goal to be achieved (goal-convergent) such as material, drawings, machinery, etc.; and also the distractions (goal-divergent).

Learning Problem. e.g. catering for very slow learners or mixed-ability groups.

Learning Programme. Any learning material or sequence of activities which has objectives and supplies information designed to lead a person to reach those objectives. Usually refers to a sequence of steps ('frames' q.v.) involving active response by the student. But this may be linear (q.v.) or branching (q.v.) and may be in printed format, tape/slide format, teaching machine (q.v.) format etc. The word 'programme' on its own is sometimes used to include also text-books, posters, films, t.v., algorithms etc.

Main characteristics are: analyses of required terminal behaviour, statement of behavioural objectives (q.v.) design of criterion test (q.v.) setting minimum test performance standards, construction of series of learning experiences, supply of knowledge of results to student, revision after trials with representative target population (q.v.).

Linear. A type of learning programme (q.v.) in which frames follow in a strict order without modification by the students' answers. Usually involves small steps compared with the large units of information given in frames of branching programmes.

Master Performer. Term used in behavioural analysis to describe someone competent in the skill being studied.

Mathetics. The systematic application of reinforcement (q.v.) theory to the analysis and reconstruction of complex behaviour (e.g. knowledge, skill). See Analysis (Behavioural).

Medium. The physical substance e.g. print, film, tape or records by means of which the 'message' is conveyed.

Monitoring. Observing acts, sounds or visuals for the purpose of reporting on performance.

Multi-media. The presenting of a variety of sensory stimuli, e.g. slide + tape + printed notes. A particular combination is called a learning system. This is a combination of elements designed to present stimuli and provide practice to enable a student to reach his objectives. The student is included in the description of the system.

Objectives. A collection of the detailed requirements for the fulfilment of a more general aim, purpose or goal of an activity. Thus *one* objective associated with the aim of developing a knowledge of spectroscopy might be to develop the student's ability to convert a wavelength to a frequency. Usually such objectives are stated in terms of what the student will DO. These are behavioural objectives, i.e. they state the desired terminal behaviour. An example might be: 'On completion of this chapter, the student should be able to convert a given wavelength into its corresponding frequency to an accuracy of 0·1 per cent, given the velocity of light in vacuo'.

Order. Position of an ability within a hierarchy of abilities or objectives relating to those abilities. Thus in Bloom's classification, the learning of knowledge is a lower-order objective than a more complex attainment such as evaluation.

Outcome. The desired learning outcome is another way of saying 'objective'.

Post-test. A criterion test (q.v.) applied after the learning experience. The difference between the results and those of the pre-test (q.v.) measure the effectiveness or 'gain' of the learning.

Prescription. A method of symbolizing complex behaviour using stimulus-response notation. Used in behavioural analysis (mathetics).

Presentation. The form in which learning material is prepared. Includes specification of media (print, film, etc.), devices (books, teaching machines, etc.) and format (learning programme, poster, case study, role playing, etc.).

Pre-test. A criterion test (q.v.) applied before the learning experience to check whether the student actually needs to learn the material. To be distinguished from the entry test (q.v.) which precedes it, and tests prerequisite skills and knowledge rather than skills and knowledge to be developed in the programme.

Prompt. Devices by means of which the probability of obtaining the correct response to a linear (q.v.) teaching frame (q.v.) is increased. Deliberate prompting must not occur in key frames of tests. Used in the theatrical sense for the act of giving aid during practice and during a performance if the person fails to recall. To be distinguished from 'cue' (q.v.). The prompt is a pedagogic device designed to shape terminal behaviour, but when the prompt's purpose has been served, to be dropped.

In branching programmes (q.v.) the several answers presented are a form of prompting, the strength of which can be increased by increasing the ease of discrimination between the correct answer and the distractors (q.v.).

Prompts in linear frames are mainly *formal* (the form of the response is indicated. A naive example is 'To live, one must eat f - - d') or *thematic,* i.e. the context suggests the answer required. A variation is the *sequence* prompt where the correct response is suggested by extrapolation from the preceding frames which are all related.

einforcement. The 'rewarding' of behaviour which is oriented towards a goal. Punishment is negative reinforcement.

In programmes, reinforcement by knowledge of results (KR) feedback to the student and a preponderance of successful responses producing a feeling of satisfaction, are considered to be the main motivational factors.

eliability. An index of the item to item consistency within a test. Measured by comparing each student's results, when the items are randomly split into two halves, in terms of a correlation coefficient. Also measured by comparing two sittings of the same or equivalent tests.

esponse. The activity initiated by some stimulus. In tests and programmes, the answers supplied by students to the items, frames etc. (stimuli).   **A.** *Constructed.* Answers thought-out and often written by the student. Used in linear learning programmes (q.v.) and short-answer test items.   **B.** *Fixed.* The list of responses is pre-determined by the examiner and known to the student. Thus the student has a multiple choice, and selects his response. Used in branching programmes (q.v.) and in most objective tests.   **C.** *Overt.* A response that is open to observation, e.g. spoken, written, drawn or selected.   **D.** *Covert.* A response that is not observable, e.g. thinking. In all cases an *active* response is thought to strengthen learning.

crambled Text. Printed version of a branching programme. The main frames are not consecutive but are scattered throughout the book. This was thought necessary in order to simulate the conditions present in teaching machines to prevent cheating.

mulation. The *real* environment for which the terminal behaviour (q.v.) is designed may be too expensive or too dangerous to use for training purposes. A substitute system is therefore devised and called a simulator. Infrequent events, such as skidding in a car or spinning in an aircraft can be programmed to happen for practice in meeting such situations. Role-playing and academic gaming are related versions which do not require machinery.

oftware. Presentation media such as print, sound, film, slides, videotape. Implies the inclusion of content, i.e. a programme on videotape rather than just a clean video tape.

em. The part of a test item in which information is given and the question is framed.

timulus. Some object or phenomenon to which we are sensitive e g. the smell of cologne, the sound of a bell, the sight of a question in a book, the feel of a hot plate, an electric shock. In general, the stimuli used in learning experiences are visual and auditory. They should, where possible, be related to the relevant stimuli present in the real situation (operational environment) in which the task being learned will eventually have to be performed.

Synthesis. Putting together the parts of the solution to a problem.

Systems. May be pedagogical, logistical, organizational or control. Pedagogical systems are concerned with learning (learning systems) Logistical systems are concerned with supplying resources (e.g. for learning-materials, staff etc.). It is one of the proclaimed aims of Educational Technology to develop systems which integrate methods and approaches, if relevant to the educational objectives determined by teachers or by society (Organizational Systems).

Control systems allow learners to progress along educational paths chosen by themselves, but suited to their abilities and development, so that an appropriate course is completed in a set period.

Systems Analysis. The detailed study of systems. Thus, in an educational context, the *systematic* development of appropriate objectives, learning experiences (materials), assessment and evaluation methods to fulfil a given function. The result is a programmed learning experience.

Target Population. The collection of students at which the learning experience (e.g. a learning programme or film) is aimed. The characteristics (e.g. age, intelligence, background, skills, knowledge, attitudes, goals) of these students will influence the design of the programme.

Taxonomy. A classification, e.g. Bloom's hierarchy of categories of educational objectives.

Teaching Machine. Mechanized book. An *adaptive* teaching machine is usually some form of computer, which presents information at a certain level of difficulty. If this produces a large student error rate, the machines lower the level of difficulty until appropriate. Similar to a branching programme. Hence, Computer Based Learning (Computer Assisted Instruction CAI).

Tests. An instrument of assessment or evaluation, e.g. an examination (attainment test usually of predetermined length, and held at the end of a course), a self-assessment test, a pre-test. Classified as Entry (q.v.), Criterion (q.v.), Section and Routing.
A. *Section Test.* To ease problems of administration, some programmes are divided into sections which together with the section tests, take a student about ½ to ¾ hour to work through. Can also be used to enter students at appropriate sections (combined with entry test).   B. *Routing Test.* Section tests with multiple choice answers, collected at the beginning of a programme. Used to route students to appropriate sections and to allow students to revise.   C. General Comments. A relevant test is one that provides the same or similar stimuli as the operational environment (real situation). Programmes or test items may themselves be tested (evaluation or validation), but this is more correctly termed a 'trial'.   D. *Objective Test.* A criterion test (q.v.) which attempts to achieve reliability by excluding subjective factors.

Training Deficiency. Difference between master performer (q.v.) and the particular student who is the target of the learning experience. The gap which the programme must bridge.

Trial Procedure. The sequence of events connected with testing out a programme or an assessment for effectiveness, on a sample of the target population. This procedure is often called 'validation', but this may confuse the concept with validity (q.v.).

The purpose of the trial is to gather data (and sometimes student's reactions) in order to check the degree to which the objectives have been reached, and to provide information, for revising programme and test if necessary. The trial does nothing to test the validity of the objectives.

Validation. (see 'trial procedure') Checking that   **A.** the programme objectives and presentation have been justified.   **B.** the various parts of the preparation and programme relate to each other, i.e. are internally consistent. In these senses, the term is more related to 'validity' than to 'trial procedure'.

Validity. A measure of the effectiveness of a test in measuring relevant characteristics; therefore, a relevant test. Usually, the effectiveness in measuring the attainment of given objectives; sometimes the usefulness or relevance of the objectives themselves. In either case virtually impossible to determine, since opinion rather than accurate measurement is involved.

APPENDIX B

List of Some Organizations Concerned with Education

ACE, Advisory Centre for Education Ltd. 32 Trumpington Street, Cambridge.
Association for Adult Education, Hon. Sec. E. W. Foulser, 28 Greenhayes Avenue, Banstead, Surrey.
Association of Education Committees, 10 Queen Anne Street, London, W.1.
Association of Educational Psychologists, Secretary, Mrs. J. Currie, 3 Grange Court, Heworth, Felling, Gateshead, Co. Durham, ME10 8EY.
APLET, Association for Programmed Learning and Educational Technology, 33 Queen Anne Street, London, W1M 0AL.
ASE, Association for Science Education, College Lane, Hatfield, Herts.
ATTI, Association of Teachers in Technical Institutions, Hamilton House, Mabledon Place, W.C.1.
AUT, Association of University Teachers, Bremar House, Sale Place, W.2.
BBC School Broadcasting Council, The Langham, Portland Place, London, W1A 1AA.
BA, British Association for the Advancement of Science, 3 Sanctuary Buildings, 20 Great Smith Street, London, S.W.1.
BACIE, British Association for Commercial and Industrial Education, 16 Park Crescent, London, W1N 4AP.
BCCE, British Committee on Chemical Education (*see* The Chemical Society).
British Council, Science Education Section, Albion House, 59 New Oxford Street, London, W.C.1.
British Federation of Film Societies, 81 Dean Street, London, W1V 6AA.
BFI, British Film Institute, 81 Dean Street, London, W1V 6AA.
British Industrial and Scientific Film Association, 193/197 Regent Street, London, W1R 7WA.
British National Film Catalogue Ltd., 193/197 Regent Street, London, W1R 7WA.
BUFC, British Universities Film Council, Royalty House, 72 Dean Street, London, W1V 5HB.
CRAC, Careers Research and Advisory Centre, Bateman Street, Cambridge.

Central Committee of Advisers in Audio Visual Education, 33 Queen Anne Street, London, W1M 0AL.

Central Committee of Teachers' Visual Aids Groups, 33 Queen Anne Street, London, W1M 0AL.

Central Film Library, Bromyard Avenue, London, W.3.

COI, Central Office of Information, Hercules House, Westminster Bridge Road, London, S.E.1.

CEDO, Centre for Educational Development Overseas, Tavistock House South, Tavistock Square, London, W.C.1.

CERI, Centre for Educational Research and Innovation (*see*OECD).

CIA, Chemical Industries Association, Alembic House, 93 Albert Embankment, London, S.E.1.

CAPITB, Chemical and Allied Products Industrial Training Board, Staines House, 158/162 Staines High Street, Staines, Middlesex.

The Chemical Society, Burlington House, Piccadilly, London, W1V 0BN. *Education Division:* Subject groups on Assessment, Curriculum, and Educational Techniques: Education and Training Board; Visual Aids Panel.

CBI, Confederation of British Industry, 21 Tothill Street, London, S.W.1.

Council for Educational Advance, Hamilton House, Mabledon Place, London, W.C.1.

CCC, Council for Cultural Cooperation, Council of Europe, Strasbourg, France.

EFVA, Educational Foundation for Visual Aids, 33 Queen Anne Street, London, W1M 0AL.

Educational Films of Scotland, 16/17 Woodside Terrace, Charing Cross, Glasgow, C.3.

ICETT, Industrial Council for Education and Training Technology, Leicester House, 8 Leicester Street, London, W.C.2.

Institute of Biology, 41 Queen's Gate, London, S.W.7.

Institute of Physics, 47 Belgrave Square, London, S.W.1.

ITB, Industrial Training Board, e.g. CAPITB.

IUPAC, International Union of Pure and Applied Chemistry, Secretariat, 2/3 Pound Way, Cowley Centre, Oxford, OX4 3YF.

ISI, Institute of Scientific Information, Mr. A. F. Cawkell, 132 High Street, Uxbridge, Middlesex.

Investigation into Supplementary Predictive Information for University Admission, Project Directorate, 19 Russell Square, London, W.C.1.

LSL, Learning Systems Ltd., Old Court House, Old Court Place, London, W.8.

Media Resources Centre, Highbury Station Road, London, N1 1SB.

National Association of Careers Teachers, Secretary, R. P. Heppell, South Shields Grammar/Technical School (Boys), South Shields, Co. Durham.

NAVAC, National Audio Visual Aids Centre, 254/256 Belsize Road, London, N.W.6.

National Audio Visual Aids Library, Paxton Place, Gipsy Road, London, S.E.27.

NAVEX, National Audio Visual Exhibition held annually at Olympia; now INTER NAVEX.

National Centre for Programmed Learning, 50 Wellington Road, Edgbaston, Birmingham 15.

NCAVAE, National Committee for Audio Visual Aids in Education, 33 Queen Anne Street, London, W1M 0AL.

NCET, National Council for Educational Technology, 160 Great Portland Street, London, W1N 5TB.

NECCTA, National Educational Closed Circuit Television Association (*see* Media Resources Centre).

NFER, National Foundation for Educational Research, The Mere, Upton Road, Slough, Bucks.

National Institute of Adult Education, 35 Queen Anne Street, London, W1M 0BL.

NIIP, National Institute for Industrial Psychology, 14 Welbeck Street, London, W1M 8DR.

National Organization for Audio Visual Aids (*see* NCAVAE).

NUS, National Union of Students, 3 Endsleigh Street, London, W.C.1.

NUT, National Union of Teachers, Hamilton House, Mabledon Place, London, WC1H 9BD.

Open University, Walton Hall, Walton, Bletchley, Bucks.

OECD, Organization for Economic Cooperation and Development, 2 rue André Pascal, Paris 16e, France.

Petroleum Films Bureau, 4 Brook Street, London, W1Y 2AY.

PICI, Programmed Instruction Centre for Industry, 32 Northumberland Park Road, Sheffield, S1O 2TX.

Royal Institution, 21 Albemarle Street, London, W.1.

Royal Society, 6 Carlton House Terrace, London, S.W.1.

Schools Council, 160 Great Portland Street, W1N 6LL.

Scottish Central Film Library, 16/17 Woodside Terrace, Glasgow, C.3.

Scottish Council for Research in Education, 46 Moray Place, Edinburgh, 3.

Scottish Educational Film Association, 16/17 Woodside Terrace, Glasgow, C.3.

Scottish Film Council, 16/17 Woodside Terrace, Glasgow, C.3.

Scottish Film Council, Industrial Panel, 16/17 Woodside Terrace, Glasgow, C.3.

Society for Education in Film and Television, 81 Dean Street, London, W1V 6AA.sb,

SRHE, Society for Research into Higher Education, 25 Northampton Square, London, EC1V 0HL.

Systems Research Ltd., Richmond, Surrey.

UKCIS, United Kingdom Chemical Information Service, The University, Nottingham, NG7 2RD.

Unit for Research into Higher Education, London School of Economics, Houghton Street, London, W.C.2.

UNESCO, United Nations Educational, Scientific and Cultural Organization Division of Science Teaching, Place de Fontenoy, Paris 7e, France.

UTMU, University Teaching Methods Unit, 55 Gordon Square, London, WC1H 0NT.

APPENDIX C

Notes on the Contributors

Ayscough, P. B. Reader in Physical Chemistry at the University of Leeds. He is interested in using computers to improve the teaching of chemistry, particularly in relation to laboratory work.

Beard, R. M. Senior Lecturer in Higher Education at the University of London, and Director of its University Teaching Methods Unit. She holds degrees in mathematics as well as in education, and is the author of numerous books on Higher Education.

Billing, D. E. Lecturer in Chemistry at Thames Polytechnic. He is interested in systematic approaches to course design and assessment methods. He was Joint Organizer of the Thames Polytechnic Conference.

Cox, R. Lecturer in the University Teaching Methods Unit of London University. He has published many papers on examination methods, and has been involved with the Inter-University Biology Project and with work on chemistry courses.

Eaborn, C. Pro-Vice-Chancellor (Science) at the University of Sussex. He is a past Chairman of the British Committee of Chemical Education and was chairman of a committee which carried out a detailed study of the relationship between university chemistry courses and the needs of industry.

Elton, L. R. B. Head of the Institute for Educational Technology and Professor of Science Education at the University of Surrey. Previously he was Head of the Department of Physics, and published work on physics education. He has carried out research on self-teaching systems, and assessment methods.

Field, B. O. Senior Lecturer in Chemistry at City University. He is interested in using programmed learning, and in improving practical courses.

Furniss, B. S. Senior Lecturer in Chemistry at Thames Polytechnic. He is interested in programmed learning, in practical courses and in pre-knowledge tests. He was joint organizer of the Thames Polytechnic Conference.

Holliday, A. K. Holder of the Grant Chair of Inorganic Chemistry at the University of Liverpool. He is investigating the teaching of chemistry at university level and the content of G.C.E. 'A' level syllabuses.

Jones, D. T. L. Principal, Redhill Technical College. He has worked on materials science and analytical instrumentation while in industry. Since moving into further education, he has been concerned with course design at all levels, and he is the author of a monograph on the education of scientists for industry.

Mackaill, A. W. Lecturer in Chemistry at Moray House College of Education, Edinburgh, and Honorary Lecturer in Chemistry at Edinburgh University. He worked on Chemical Education for his Ph.D., and has published several papers on assessment in chemistry.

Roberts, I. F. Senior Lecturer in Education at the University of Keele where he has been concerned with the development of the joint honours course in Mathematics and Science Education. He is also co-author of a standard text on Further Education.

Ronayne, J. Lecturer in the Department of Liberal Studies in Science at the University of Manchester. A former lecturer in organic chemistry at Wolverhampton Polytechnic, he is now interested in the development of broad based courses in science, in the dissemination of information in chemistry and in problems of science policy.

Tatchell, A. R. Head of the Division of Organic Chemistry at Thames Polytechnic. He is interested in the use of television to teach practical skills and has been involved with making two series of television programmes for transmission on the London ETV network.

APPENDIX D

Answers to Text Questions

Answers to the questions asked about objectives on p. 12:

Yes, behavioural: *b, d, e, h*;
No, not behavioural: *a, c, f, g.*

Answers to the test on pp. 75-76.
1. C
2. B, C, F, G
3. B
4. All